LIFE WITH THE BARK ON

BY EARL EASTHAM

Life With The Bark On
Earl A. Eastham

Published By Parables
February, 2021

All Rights Reserved. No part of this book may be reproduced or utilized in any form or by any means, electronic or mechanical, including photocopying, recording, or by any information storage and retrieval system, without permission in writing from the author.

ISBN 9781951497439
Printed in the United States of America

Readers should be aware that Internet Web sites offered as citations and/or sources for further information may have been changed or disappeared between the time this was written and the time it is read.

Life With The Bark On

By Earl A. Eastham

Foreword

In the year September 1945 America ...and much of the rest of the World...had just completed a long and bloody war. It had to be fought with rifles, tanks, planes, bombs, and the like. It had cost the United States the lives of thousands of her young men and women. It had left many more thousands wounded and no longer able to work. Rural America changed as country populations moved to the cities to replace the loss of manpower. The development of the atomic bomb by an American Scientist was extremely instrumental in ending the war.

Principally during the 1940s and 1950s, America ...again also much of the World... was fighting another war. The enemy this time was Infantile Paralysis or Poliomyelitis, commonly called Polio. It was fought with drugs, medical care by most. Some also added a good mental attitude, humor, and faith in God. It cost the United States the lives of many of her children. It left many paralyzed. The development of the Polio vaccine by an American Scientist was instrumental in defeating Polio but was not developed until 1955 and later perfected in 1961.

This book is about a child that fought this enemy in 1946, years before final victory was declared. A large portion of this story is based on real life events that actually happened. All names were changed or invented for the sake of the story.

Table Of Contents

Chapter One	5
The Setting	
Chapter Two	17
Day 1: [Sat.] The Infection	
Chapter Three	23
Day 5: [Wed.] To The Doctor	
Chapter Four	29
Day 12: [Wed.] Pt.1 Return To The Doctor	
Chapter Five	35
Day 12: [Wed.] Pt. 2 Intro. To The Hospital	
Chapter Six	39
Day 13: [Thur.] Polio Official	
Chapter Seven	49
Day 20: [Thur.] Four Eyes	
Chapter Eight	57
Day 22: [Sat.] Aunt Lolla Bell	
Chapter Nine	67
Day 24: [Mon.] Hospital Food & Updating Mother	
Chapter Ten	79
Day 27: [Thur.] Meeting Polly	
Chapter Eleven	91
Day 29: [Sat.] Biggest Liar In East Texas	
Chapter Twelve	109
Day 31: [Mon.] Filling In Mother	
Chapter Thirteen	119
Day 34: [Thur.] Fathers Explained	
Chapter Fourteen	133
Day 36: [Sat.] Visits: Best & Worst	
Chapter Fifteen	145
Day 38: [Mon.] Forty Questions: Sleep Best & Worst	

Chapter Sixteen	161
Day 41: [Thur.] Intro to Iron Lung	
Chapter Seventeen	171
Day 62: [Thur.] Polly Returns	
Chapter Eighteen	183
Day 63: [Fri.] The Preacher & The Whittler	
Chapter Nineteen	201
Day 67: [Tues.] The Death Revelation	
Chapter Twenty	213
Day 68: [Wed.] The Signing, Going Home	
Chapter Twenty-One	229
Day 69: [Thur.] First Day Home	
Chapter Twenty-Two	235
Day 70: [Fri.] The Kids Come Home	
Chapter Twenty-Three	245
Day 81: [Tues.] The Bark Is Removed	

Life With The Bark On

Chapter One
The Setting

"AHHIIIIEEEEOOOHOW!!!" Adrian howled. At each smack of the paddle on his bottom he let out another howl. While it truly hurt, as it was supposed to do, he added a little to the howl for extra sound effect. His mother completed the distasteful chore that neither of them enjoyed.

Adrian decided life was rough on a kid. Adrian was really sorry for what he had done and knew he had been wrong. He had indeed, been a bad boy. Wiping the tears from his eyes and rubbing his bottom, he recalled the events that led up to this unpleasant correction. Adrian was a very active boy. He did not like to be still for any length of time especially a long time.

He had decided he wanted to play cowboys. He just loved playing cowboys. It was his favorite game. Of course, he was always the good guy, in fact the hero. Now everybody knows if you are going to play cowboys, you need some related equipment.

He had found his toy pistol he had gotten a couple of Christmases ago in a set. It had been a humdinger of a set. Since then, the holster had been lost in the family's last move. The gun was missing the cylinder since his little brother, Lee had decided to beat on it with an old hammer. But, no matter, it would do. He had stuck the gun in his belt.

Being a boy used to using his imagination when at play, he needed his stick horse, whom he had named Old Paint, but it had gotten run over by the family car when Adrian had left it in the driveway overnight. Secretly, he believed he was getting too old to play with stick horses. However, Lee had a perfectly good, only slightly worn, stick horse. Adrian reasoned that if a stick horse was available, why not use it.

It was at this point that Adrian made the decision that got him into trouble. He felt that, as the older brother, Lee should let him use Lee's stick horse. Now Lee called his horse Blacky, who could not run as fast as Old Paint...because Lee's legs were shorter..., and was actually 2 inches shorter; but it would do. Adrian knew he should have asked Lee if he could borrow it, but he did not ask. He just went and took it. When Lee loudly objected, Adrian shoved Lee aside and took it anyway and ran outside to play.

He usually played together with Lee. In fact, Adrian figured if all the imaginary bad guys and bad Indians he and Lee had shot were laid side by side, they would cover about a quarter of Houston. But, hey, there was only one stick horse.

Of course, Lee ran and told their mother on Adrian. She had to interrupt her day of busy household chores and call Adrian in from play. "Adrian Phillip North, you come here this instant," said his mother, in a tired but loud voice. Adrian knew he was in big trouble, especially when he heard his full name.

Adrian knew what he had done was wrong. He really wanted to be a good boy, but it was not always so easy. He left the stick horse outside and came into the room. He saw Lee standing there with tears in his eyes and gave him a not so kind look.

"Did you take your brother's stick horse without getting his permission?" Mother demanded.

"Yes Mother," Adrian answered. He knew better than to lie.

"Did you shove him down?" his mother continued.

"Well, yes Mother," said Adrian in answer.

"Why did you do that?" She demanded.

"Well, you see, Old Paint, my stick horse was broken and Lee was not using his. I really needed a good stick horse," Adrian answered in what he felt was his most logical tone. He quickly realized it was doing him no good. He could see his mother was not buying it. Adrian realized his mother was preparing for the part of the correction process that he really dreaded, almost more than the spanking. It was what he called **The Lecture**.

Adrian's mother took the raising of her children very seriously. She believed that it was in their formative years that they needed to be taught the difference between right and wrong. If the offense was serious enough, then the correction should also include physical punishment.

The North's believed the Bible taught that foolishness was bound up in the heart of a child. Adrian figured what that meant was, that what a kid thought was fun and right was what grownups often thought was foolishness, and even being bad. From past experience he believed he must have a lot of foolishness in him.

His parents also said the Bible said the rod of

correction would drive it from the kid. He was not real sure what the rod meant, but he was pretty sure his parents believed it included his dad's belt, or some kind a paddle.

He did remember once when Ann, Adrian's little sister, got into trouble. At that time, his mother could not find a paddle handy, so she told Ann to go out into the yard and bring her a switch off the tree, a weeping willow tree. Ann asked what a switch was and mother said in exasperation, "A limb." Ann returned with a large limb. It was so big she had to drag it. The sight of this little girl so innocently bringing such a limb for her own spanking, cracked her mother up. That was one time that Ann was spared a spanking and she did not even realize why.

Mother believed a spanking was to be applied in the proper fashion to the proper place. In other words, a spanking on the bottom. She said God had prepared a padded place that blows would not damage anything but still inflict enough pain to get the message across.

Mother had what some call "an old school philosophy of child rearing". She believed that parents are always teaching their children as much as by what they did as what they didn't do. She believed that for most children, much of life's attitudes and values are learned from their parents in those early, formative years.

She believed that if you just yell at a child, they soon learn that your correction has no real pain, so it does not mean much. Some children even learn that they can yell back and still not be truly punished. Also, if a parent threatens a punishment and does not deliver, that teaches a child you don't mean what you say. For example: a child is acting up in a grocery store and being embarrassing to the parents, and it is not proper or convenient to correct them then, and you promise correction when you get home. Then later when you get them home you do not deliver the correction, for whatever reason. Maybe you are both tired or perhaps the infraction does not seem so bad, or even forgotten. You have taught them that your threat was empty, or you did not mean it. You have broken your word, or worse yet, that you have lied.

She also believed that if you tell a child you are going to do some terrible thing that they know you are never going to do; you have taught them that you make empty threats. For example, don't tell a child you are going to slap their face if you have no intention of hitting a child in the face. Or, don't tell a child that you are going to nail their foot to the floor if they don't stand still. You have made an empty threat and they know it.

Once Adrian thought his mom had made an empty threat. She said if she ever heard him say a cuss word, she would wash his mouth out with soap. Surely, she would not be that drastic. However, when he said a word he had heard at school and he knew it was a bad word, he learned his Mother did not make empty threats. Mother took a washrag, soaped it up, and proceeded to wipe it around in his mouth. It really did not hurt him, but it certainly drove the point home. He would get the taste of soap in his mouth ever after, when he said a cuss word.

As the mother of four small children, one of which was only a year old, she really had more than enough to do. However, correction was also of major importance. Also, she had the wisdom not to spank out of anger. Adrian's mother told him to stand right where he was and don't move. She then began to calm herself down. She made sure Lee was playing quietly in the corner, younger sister Ann was put into a playpen, which she was really too big for, and the baby was put into his crib.

Since Adrian had been ordered to stand right where he was, he could not try to pull the stunt he had tried a few weeks earlier. He had been about to get a spanking. But while his mother was securing the evening meal and seeing to the other children in preparation for his punishment, he had run to his room. He quickly put on three pairs of underwear under his jeans. He reasoned this would pad the blows. He knew his mother never spanked except in the proper area. His father was not always so careful with his aim. That stunt backfired on him, however. In her wisdom and experience, she quickly deduced his hasty preparation. The fact that his jeans did not button or zip all the way up probably had a lot to do with giving him away. His mother's creative solution was to make him take off everything except one pair of underwear and receive his spanking so shamefully clad. The humility and lack of cloth covering made that spanking seem especially painful. He proposed not to try that stunt again.

Then started the rough part, **The Lecture**. His mother said, "Son, you know that your mother loves you. What she does not love is when you are bad and do mean and hurtful things. I am sure you know that taking other people's stuff without asking is wrong. In fact, it really is stealing. Just because you want it really bad and are bigger than your brother and can take it, is no excuse for taking his things. Also shoving him down is mean. You would not really like it if someone did that kind of thing to you would you; especially if they were bigger than you?" she asked.

"No Mother," he shamefully replied.

"Also," Mother continued, "When you are bad, it hurts your father, and me, and Jesus."

When she put it like that what could he say? "No mother," he said as he started to sob. Now he was even more sorry. He really did want to be a good boy. He <u>also</u> really did not want to get the spanking.

"I really am sorry mother (sob), and I promise I want do it again. (sob) Do I still have to get the spanking?" He had figured he did, but it never hurt to try.

"Yes, you do, you must learn that all decisions have consequences. Bad decisions have bad consequences. All wrong results in punishment sooner or later. First if I tell you, you are going to get a spanking and don't give it to you, then I have told you a lie. Then I have done wrong. Second, spanking helps us to learn that doing wrong is really serious," Mother finished, with a sigh.

Mother had sat down and brought out a big old wooden stirring spoon that had a double life. It stirred the family food, but it was also the rod of correction. Father preferred to use his leather belt.

Adrian trudged wearily back to the sleeping cabin. The Norths lived in two cabins in a part-time motel. Most units were for rent by the night. Others by the week or month. Mr. North had wanted to get in closer to the city. For the last year and eight months, they had had to live in a farmhouse near the city. Adrian's father had lost his job and had moved his family into the farm house for what was to be a temporary solution. It had given Adrian some experiences that he would doubtless remember the rest of his life. Father had decided to try the motel by the month till he could find something better that he could afford. He rented two cabins: one for the family to sleep in and the other to cook and eat in.

Adrian was glad they both had bathrooms. The farm house in the country only had an outhouse. Actually, it was not really an outhouse in the standard sense of the word. It was an old goat shed. His father, being a country boy used to making do with what he had, had converted it. He put a door in the side with new hinges. He put a board across one side of the building, just the right height to sit on. It had a board coming up from the floor to support the seat and prevent any waste splashing on one's feet. All you had to do was be sure to sit far enough back to do your business. Mother had a recent Sears catalog to take care of the paperwork.

The cabins were all alike. They were surrounding a sort of square. Adrian thought they all could use a coat of paint. In his eyes, a better color or even using a brighter white, would be a vast improvement. But then, who paid attention to what a kid thought? Certainly not cheap motel owners. The cars had a small parking place in front of each cabin.

The owner of the motel employed a couple named Peavey, to keep up the motel and grounds. Mrs. Peavey was supposed to clean the inside of the cabins every time a guest moved out. She did a reasonably good job.

Mr. Peavey was supposed to fix things up and keep up the grounds. To say the least, he left a lot to be desired. His saying was "Why do today what you can put off till tomorrow?" He boasted he was the plumber, the electrician, groundskeeper, and chief bottle washer. Adrian never understood that last part. He had never seen Mr. Peavey wash one bottle. Mr. Peavey seemed to be more interested in a different small flat bottle, which he brought out when he thought no one was looking.

In the summer, Mr. Peavey let what little grass there was to get about six inches high before he mowed. Then he complained it was the mower's fault and the mower was no good to cut what he called, a few slightly high weeds. After all, he could not be expected to be out mowing the yard every day or two. He was only one man and a busy man with lots of responsibility at that.

There was always some light bulb out in the lights outside the front of each cabin or in the parking lot. The neon sign on the road that told of the motel's name should have read:

SANDY'S
HANDY
DANDY
MOTEL
NO VACANCY

A lot of the time it read

ANDY AND DAN MOT NO CAN

Adrian thought Mr. Peavey was more than a little afraid to climb his very rickety old ladder. Most every Saturday, he made the rounds in an ancient Ford pickup truck. The garbage cans were usually overflowing by Saturday. He picked up most of the larger pieces and bags of garbage. If the neighborhood dogs had torn the bags and spread out the smaller pieces of garbage, or the wind scattered it, then that garbage had to wait till he got around to raking the grounds. To his credit he got around to raking the grounds about once a month. To hear him tell it, he ran a high-class operation.

Of course, the owner had to share the blame for not purchasing the neon bulbs to replace the bulbs on the sign.

The rest of the day the North household was relatively calm and uneventful. A situation for which Mrs. North was really grateful. Four children and household chores caused her to cherish any quiet and peaceful time she could get.

Later that night, Adrian knelt down beside his bed to say his prayers. He literally said prayers, not just a prayer. The way he figured it was best to cover all the bases. First, he said the Lord's prayer which he had learned in Sunday School.

Our Father who art in heaven,

Hallowed be thy name.
Thy kingdom come,
Thy will be done.
On Earth as it is in Heaven,
Give us this day our daily bread.
And forgive us our debts,
As we forgive our debtors.
And lead us not into temptation,
But deliver us from evil.
For thine is the Kingdom, and the power,
and the Glory, for ever and ever. Amen.

Next Adrian said the "Lay Me Down to Sleep" prayer his parents had taught him.

Lay me down to sleep,
I pray the Lord my soul to keep.
If I die before I wake,
I pray the Lord my soul to take.
If I live for other days,
I pray the Lord to guide my ways. Amen.

Finally, Adrian prayed what he called "cover the other stuff prayer."

Dear Jesus please bless Mother and Father,
And Lee, and Ann, and Baby Edmond.
Please forgive me for the bad things I did today,
I really am sorry Jesus.
Please help me be a good boy,
I don't know why I keep doing bad stuff.

Please help all the little children,
On the mission field,
And heal all the sick people.
And save all the people
That don't know you.
(Like Mr. Peavey)
I know you forgave all my sins,
When I gave my life over to you.
Please forgive me the sins,
I done did since then.
In Jesus name, Amen
Oh yeah and Jesus,
Please help me get another stick horse.
Amen

Adrian crawled into bed, and was soon fast asleep.

Chapter Two
Day One: [Sat.] The Infection

Adrian woke to a real dreary day. It looked like he was going to be cooped up in the small motel cabin all day. For an active boy, that was a kind of torture all of its own.

Outside the steady light rain from all night had turned the area in front and between the cabins into a sea of mud. A constant flow of transient traffic, the flow of people and cars kept the area churned up year 'round. Dust in the summer and mud in the winter. Only one other cabin was a monthly rental at the time. It was on the other side of the square. An older couple rented it. They had no children the North children could play with. The rest of the motel stayed booked up with over niter's, most of the year round.

Adrian felt he had a dilemma. It was true that he wanted to be obedient to his mother. He had been instructed to stay inside today and watch Lee. However, he did not feel like being a babysitter. Also, Lee was big enough to watch out for himself, Adrian reasoned.

The memory of yesterday's punishment was still fresh on his mind. However, he was really bored. The idea of playing in the rain and getting that wonderful mud squishing between his toes was a temptation almost too great to forgo. Being raised a country boy, he never wore shoes unless he had to.

The more he thought about it, the more he convinced himself that surely there might just be something his mother needed in the other cabin. Maybe something had come up since she left a couple of hours ago that she had not thought of at the time. Perhaps he should run over and check with her.

For a while he stood with the cabin door slightly open, looking outside. He persuaded himself that it would be a helpful and caring boy that thought of his mother's needs so much. Now, if he just happened to run through some mud going or coming that would be just unpreventable great fun. What harm could it do? After all, isn't a guy entitled to make the best out of a situation, and to have a little fun out of life? You could almost see the battle going on in Adrian's head as he struggled with what he knew he should do and what he wanted to do.

Adrian made up his mind. He would go. Having made that decision, all sorts of reasons and excuses for doing it seemed to fit with his doing what he really wanted to do. Caution fell by the wayside. He got up and put on his practically new raincoat which included a great rain hat. Mother had got it just a couple weeks ago from the Goodwill store. It was a little big, but who cared? He ordered Lee to continue to play and that he would be right back.

"You are going to get into trouble again. Mother told us to stay inside today." Lee warned.

"You stay inside and be quiet. I will be right back before you know it," threatened Adrian. He opened the door and slipped outside. What fun! He really enjoyed the run through the mud to the other cabin. He went fairly straight over to the other cabin the North's had rented. He went right in and asked his mother, with all innocence, if there was anything, he could do for her or anything she needed that he could get for her.

She saw right through his ploy. She also did not appreciate the muddy footprints he left on her clean floor.

"Young man, you get back over to the other cabin this minute. And this time stay inside. Do you hear me?" Mother sternly ordered.

"I expected you to watch your brother, not to run around in the rain and track mud all over my clean floors. The first thing I know you will be coming down with a cold or something. And wash your feet and clean up the floor when you get back over there. Do you hear me?" she demanded.

"Yes Mother," Adrian answered sheepishly. He closed the door behind him and started back across to the other cabin.

I was just trying to be helpful, he thought. He was trying to justify his actions in his own mind. The mud again felt good, in fact delightful, on his feet and between his toes. He decided that since he would not get another chance like this for a long time, and besides his feet were already muddy, why not enjoy it while he could?

He made a big circle then a loop-t-loop. This was great fun, so he made another one, then another. He added some war whoops as he ran. As he made that last loop-t-loop, he tripped over a stone covered by mud. He fell flat on his face into the mud, with his mouth wide open over some garbage, thanks to the dogs and Mr. Peavey. Rain, mud, and garbage all went into his open mouth. It also got into his nose and one eye. He staggered up, sputtering, and trying to spit. He felt he was too big a boy to cry, although he sure felt like it. Both his hands were covered in mud, so he could not even wipe his face, as it would only spread the mess. He could just barely see well enough to get back to the cabin.

When Adrian entered the cabin; Lee took one look at him and asked, "What happened to you? You look a mess!"

Adrian answered with "Mind your own business!"

"I am going to tell Mother on you," Lee threatened.

"You do and I will punch you in the mouth," Adrian threatened in return. He went to the sink and began the cleaning up. It took quite a while to get the mud off his face and hands. His left eye burned some, but he could see well enough to finish the cleaning up. He also washed his feet. The nasty taste in his mouth and burning in his nose would not go away even after rinsing them several times.

Then came the cleaning of the raincoat. The rain hat had disappeared but he was not going back outside to look for it. Also, he had to change his pants and shirt.

Next, he cleaned up all the muddy hand and foot prints They were all over the room, it seemed. All this cleaning up job took more than twice as long as he had spent outside, "having fun." It did not help to have Lee sitting there grinning. Not saying anything, just grinning. The thought went through Adrian's mind that he ought to go punch him anyway. He immediately felt guilty because actually Lee was his best friend and he really loved his little brother.

Mother came in a short time after Adrian had finished cleaning up. She took one look around and as wise mothers so often do, did not have to ask what had happened.

Besides she had seen the footprints of the loop-t-loop and found the rain hat.

All mother said was; "I hope you have learned a lesson young man," She then called Adrian to her and washed some of the mud out of his hair and behind his ears that he had missed. She decided that all that cleaning up of the mess had been punishment enough.

Lee piped up, "I didn't do anything Mother, it was all Adrian." Lee figured he would score some points for good behavior.

"Well see that you don't," warned Mother. Knowing boys, she realized that given half a chance, Lee would have been out there with Adrian. In fact, half the trouble Lee got into was following the misdeeds of his older brother.

Adrian gave Lee a hard look then said: "Mother, I am kind of tired. I want to take a nap until supper."

"OK son," Mother tenderly replied.

Somehow the fun that he had enjoyed hardly seemed worth it now. Maybe that was the lesson Mother had said he should have learned. Sometimes grownups said things that he only partly understood. Mostly, lessons were what you did in school. He guessed, however, that you could learn stuff from what happens to you, and that is kind of like a lesson. Mother had also said he tried to think too much, whatever that meant.

That night Adrian asked to be excused from the table after supper and announced he wanted to go to bed.

Father commented, "What is wrong with him? Aren't some of his favorite radio programs are on tonight? Let's see he likes **The Lone Ranger, Batman, The Shadow, and Flash Gordon**. After all, this is 1946, the modern age of radio. We did not have that when I was growing up. I know he hardly ever wants to miss any one of those four."

"Yes, I know dear," patiently replied Mother. Actually, he had a rather rough time this afternoon. I will tell you all about it after we get the kids to bed."

"Don't forget to say your prayers, young man!" Father called as Adrian opened the door to carefully return to the sleeping cabin.

"Yes Sir," answered Adrian.

In bed he said his prayers. He liked to do that after he was in bed instead of kneeling beside the bed. That always hurt his knees. Father said the important thing was to say them...not what position you were in when you said them.

In his "cover other stuff" prayer, he prayed:

I love you Lord Jesus.
I am really sorry I was bad
And played in the rain and mud today
After Mother told me to stay inside.
I am sorry I got mad a Lee
I don't feel so good, so please make me better.
Bless my whole family.
In Jesus name, Amen.

Chapter Three
Day Five: [Wed.] To the Doctor

Adrian woke again feeling terrible. The North children were seldom seriously ill. Mother had an old country cure she used on her children every year that kept them reasonably healthy. First of all, she prayed for them and their health all the time. However, every summer she brought out the Syrup of Black Draught.

Every summer, so as not to interfere with school, for a week she gave all the children a spoon full, twice each day. She did this religiously whether they acted sick or not. Her mother had used this cure on her and her siblings, so if it was good enough for them it was good enough for her kids.

Now this was a strong laxative, and boy, did it work. After a week, a germ would not even think of staying in a body. You did not play too hard, and no one got too far from the bathroom. The stuff tasted awful. All but the baby dreaded the Black Draught week. So far, he was not old enough to "enjoy" the torture of Black Draught Week.

If Mother could not get Black Draught, she had a backup called Castor Oil. It also could be used as a laxative but, hard as it is to believe, it tasted worse than Black Drought. It could also be used for dry skin, since it was an oil. When Mother rubbed it all over the kids, Father said they looked like a bunch of greased pigs.

Adrian had never seen a bunch of greased pigs, but he thought that would be a real sight. Father said they had a sport in the country of trying to see how many greased pigs one could catch in a limited time. Now a pig would be hard enough to catch without being greased, Adrian thought. However, to add grease would seem to make it next to impossible Adrian believed. But Father said he had caught one or two in his day.

Adrian had not felt well since he had played in the rain. At first his parents had thought he had just got a very bad cold. They had started giving him some over-the-counter cold medicine. Also, he took some cough drops they had around the cabin. For a day or two he seemed to be getting better, but then he took a turn for the worse. They began to think that he might be seriously ill. Adrian had started to have trouble breathing and coughing a lot more. He was making a "whooping" sound when he coughed. Mother got Aunt Stella May to watch the rest of the children and took Adrian to the doctor. Aunt Stella May was Mother's younger sister. She had been living in the city for some time. She had five kids of her own.

It was late in the day when the North's got to Dr. Hickory's Office. Dr Hickory had been the North's family doctor since they came to the city. Believe it or not, Adrian's earliest memory of Dr. Hickory was when the doctor circumcising him. Adrian was almost four years old when his parents had it done. It was a painful memory for him. That was old to be circumcised. He had been told that most children have it done shortly after birth but his was when he was three. He was never told why. He suspected that while it had health reasons, it also had some religious reasons. Dr. Hickory was a kindly General Practitioner, in his sixties. He handled everything from delivering babies (he had delivered Edmond) to setting broken bones, to fatal diseases. He had been in general practice for thirty-five years. That did not include two tours of duty as an army doctor in the Great War.

The waiting room was crowded, as it had been all day. Adrian's parents had not made an appointment, but the receptionist knew the family and could see that Adrian was really sick. She said, if at all possible, she would work them in somehow.

As it worked out, Adrian was the last patient of the day. The head nurse, Nurse Peabody, had locked the front door forty-five minutes ago. The office would be closed for the next three days. All the staff in the office were looking forward to some time off. Dr. Hickory had a peaceful fishing trip planned with his grandson. They had been planning it for weeks. He needed some R. & R. and some bonding time with his grandson, who by the way, was named after him.

The good doctor planned to start bright and early the very next day and go to this little hidden lake he knew about. One could fish off the pier or out in a boat, as one chose. The lake was full of fish according to the last report. Bait was plentiful this time of year, and the weather was perfect.

Mother went with Adrian to the examining room. The doctor listened to her as she described how Adrian had been feeling sick and his many symptoms. As the

Doctor started the examination, Adrian started to have a spell of his whoop sounding cough. The doctor thought it could be several things. His training told him to run some tests.

Had he not been so tired, and with more time, Dr. Hickory would have made a more careful decision. In his tiredness, he could hear those trout and bass jumping.

To Adrian's mother, the doctor said, "I think this young fellow has what appears to be "Whooping Cough". Here are some pills you can start him on. Give him one every four hours. Keep him quiet, with lots of liquids and plenty of rest. He needs to be isolated from the rest of the family as much as possible. This could be contagious. Oh, and see he gets as much fresh air as possible. I want to see him again in four or five days. Make an appointment with Sara on your way out."

"Thank you, Dr. Hickory." Mother said as she took Adrian back to the now empty waiting room.

The doctor dropped tiredly into a chair and reached for a notepad. He quickly made notes in long hand for Adrian's file. His niece, the receptionist Sara, would type them up later. At last, he could get a little time off. In his mind, he was already out on that lake pulling in record trout.

Mother made an appointment for six days later.

Adrian tried to remember when he had felt this sick before. The **Jello Caper** came to mind as being fairly close. While living on the farm, Mother made two large bowls of Jello, enough to last a couple of days. It was an inexpensive dessert for a poor family's budget. Adrian had gotten really greedy. When he had as many helpings as remained in the bowl mother had fixed for that evening, he still wanted more. He began to ask the other children if they were going to eat all of theirs, and if not could, he have it. He was what his father called "making a pig of himself".

Father made the decision to teach Adrian a life lesson. He had Mother get the other bowl out of the ice box and put it on the table. He then told Adrian to start eating. Now when you are doing something you want to do, it is one thing. However, when you get caught and <u>have</u> to do it, that's another thing altogether. That pleasurable thing can suddenly become not near as good or fun as it once was. That whole bowl of Jello now looked gigantic.

Adrian knew his father meant business and in no way would he try to argue or disobey. But after two more heaping bowls of Jello, he began to feel very sick of Jello. His father dipped up the third bowl. Adrian ate a couple of lot smaller bites than he had previously had and felt he was going to throw up. It did not help the situation that his siblings were sitting there staring at him. Father knew that the lesson was not lost on them.

Father asked Adrian if he thought he had enough?

Adrian answered "Yes Sir, I am sure I have."

Father then asked Adrian if he thought he was going to make a pig of himself ever again?

"No Sir, can I be excused from the table now?" he pleaded.

Adrian remembered that he had been very sick. He never could stand Jello again. He could hardly stand the sight of it. Much to his horror, he was soon to learn that the main dessert served in hospitals is always Jello.

Adrian made a short "other stuff" prayer that night. He quickly prayed:

> *Dear Lord Jesus please help me*
> *To get well really quick.*
> *Bless Mother and Father and*
> *Lee, Ann, and the Baby*
> *Oh Yeah Edmond,*
> *And all the missionary kids*
> *All over the world*
> *Please forgive me'*
> *All the times I sin.*
> *Amen.*

It did not take Adrian long to go to sleep that night.

Chapter Four
Day 12: [Wed.] Pt.1 Return To The Doctor

Father, Mother, and Adrian were again on the way to the doctor's office. The other children were again with Aunt Stella May. This was serious enough that Father had taken another day off from work He could lose his job with too many days off, but this was a matter of priority. It was about 9 am and shortly after rush hour. Father still hated the rush hour traffic in the city. They got stuck in it their last trip to the doctor.

Father carried Adrian into the doctor's office, because Adrian was too weak to walk. His 115 pounds was no problem for his big, strong dad.

When Sara, the receptionist, saw how sick Adrian looked she said, "Mr. North, take him right on back and put him on the bed in examining room number four. It's right down the hall, second door to the left."

Nurse Peabody came in with Adrian's chart. She took his blood pressure, pulse, and temperature and logged it on the chart. She then stuck it in a holder on the door.

"You can both wait in here," she said to Adrian's parents. "The doctor will be with you shortly."

Father said. "They do that in every doctor's office in the world no matter what the language or country."

"Do what?" asked mother.

"Take your blood pressure, pulse, and temperature and leave saying the doctor will be with you in a minute."

"Oh You!" mother said, sort of scolding.

Nurse Peabody returned shortly with Dr. Hickory. The doctor, while somewhat rested, was already caught up in a busy caseload. He had really enjoyed the weekend with his grandson fishing. They had caught a good mess of fish and cooked and ate their catch. Even the downpour of rain Sunday evening as they were heading back to the city did not really dampen their spirits.

The doctor took a quick look at Adrian's chart and then, putting on a pair of blue plastic gloves, he began a closer examination of Adrian himself.

"Hum! Hum!" he kept saying, to nobody in particular, as he looked at Adrian's throat. With a swab, he took a sample from Adrian's throat and put it in a glass vile. Next, he then took a sample of the stuff running from Adrian's nose and put that into a vile.

"Nurse Peabody, send these next door to the lab immediately, along with a blood sample. Tell them I want a diagnosis, Stat." He took a form and checked some items on it and handed it to her.

Turning to the Norths, he said, "This may take a little while, but I don't want you to go anywhere. I have a lot of influence in that lab, so they will hurry. I am afraid our boy Adrian here is a really sick boy."

Adrian shut his eyes and looked the other way

when Nurse Peabody stuck a needle in his arm to draw blood. He looked like he wanted to cry, but did not,

"See Mother, I am a big boy. I didn't even cry, although that hurt something awful"

Mother turned her head away and looked like she was about to cry.

"Yes, you are a big boy," his father said tenderly.

The lab was attached to the same building, but with a separate entrance. It had state of the art equipment for the time, being a small independent lab. Dr. Hickory was one of the principal owners, so the work he sent over usually got number one priority handling. They got right to work on his samples.

A messenger came over from the lab in less than an hour and a half with the results of the tests Dr. Hickory had asked for. He looked over the results and did his "Hum" thing again. He reentered the examination room and started looking over Adrian, again. He put that cold stethoscope thing on Adrian's chest again and told him to cough. In his present state, Adrian obliged with several coughs at a time.

The doctor did more of the "Hum". He tried not to look undecided. He just was not positive. From the lab results and his own examination, it could be either Diphtheria or Polio. Being a concerned doctor and friend of these folks, he wanted to give them the best news possible. The lesser of two evils, as it were.

Dr. Hickory cleared his throat and looked seriously at the parents. "I must tell you Adrian is a very sick boy. I believe he has Diphtheria. He needs to be in the hospital right away. I know you don't have insurance, so you had better take him to the county hospital. They will admit him. I will call them now. They will admit him to the emergency as soon as you get there."

"Do you know where the county hospital is? Also, do you know the best route to get there?" asked Dr. Hickory.

"Yes, to both questions doctor. And, thank you," Father said.

"Honey!" he said to Mother. "I will put Adrian in the car. Will you pick up the bill?"

"Of course!" she replied.

Father hurriedly scooped up Adrian and headed for the car while Mother spoke to Sara.

"We will send a check as soon as we can," she sort of sheepishly explained.

"We know that. You always do," Sara answered with looks of real sympathy in her eyes.

In the car, Mother asked Adrian, trying to take his mind off his condition, "You are always such a big talker and thinker why are you so quiet, son?"

"I really don't feel like talking Mother, but I do have a question?" Adrian replied.

"You usually do," remarked his father.

"Mother, you said that all actions have consequences. Is my being bad the reason I got sick? Is God punishing me because I have been especially bad here lately. I know I have not behaved at all well since we moved into the cabins. It is true they are nicer than the farmhouse where we last lived, in lots of ways, but I really still don't like them. I was hoping Father would find us a real house to live in soon."

"Let me answer this," Father said to Mother. I know the Cabins are crowded and not what we are really looking for. It has been hard on you kids. I understand why you feel all cooped up, especially in bad weather. Your Mother and I also feel cooped up. I am looking as hard as I can to find us a nice house we can afford. I believe my new job will give us the money to find a better place real soon. I am trying as hard as I can," Father repeated. But let me tell you, God is not punishing you with this sickness. He just does not do that. I don't know why or how you got sick, but God does not punish little boys with sickness for misbehaving."

"Father, I also have to confess that the other day I got out and played in the rain. Also, I fell down and got all muddy and then tracked it into the cabin. I spent hours cleaning it all up. I also argued with Lee and threatened him not to tell."

To Mother, Father said, "Why is this the first I am hearing about this?"

"Well, I figured that all the trouble he had to go to, to clean up himself and how bad he already felt, was punishment enough." Mother answered.

"Not the way I would have handled it, but I understand your reasoning," Father commented.

Having confessed, Adrian felt better in his heart, but in his body, he felt really lousy. They were soon arriving at the hospital and it was one of the biggest and most frightening buildings that Adrian felt he had ever seen. There also seemed to be lots and lots of cars and lots of people.

An ambulance came charging by them with a police car escort, sirens blaring. Father had to pull out of the way to let them pass. They went further down to the entrance which had a large sign with large red letters that proclaimed it was the emergency entrance.

"I guess we need to go down to that entrance as well. Dr. Hickory did not specify emergency, but I believe that is the most logical place to check in," commented Father. "You park the car while I carry Adrian inside. As busy as they are, I will probably still be waiting by the time you get the car parked and get in there. Be sure to watch out for private spaces reserved for doctors and the like. I have been told they have special parking spaces for everyone and his dog."

Chapter Five
Day 12: [Wed.] Pt. 2 Introduction to the Hospital

The county had built this hospital for just such people as the North's. It served the needs of the poor of such a big city and the surrounding towns. You were not turned away because you had no insurance or money. The county covered most of the cost. True, it did not have some of the most advanced equipment the big private hospitals had. In fact, some of its equipment was well worn. Also, most of the big-name doctors practiced at the private hospitals. However, government and private grants supplemented the county funding. Like all such institutions, it served the needs of the big county of which the large city of Houston covered most. The population was expanding very rapidly. Also, like all such institutions, the funding never seemed to quite cover all the needs the staff felt it should have.

The general population referred to the hospital as the Charity Hospital, when, in actuality, its official name was Harris County General Hospital.

The doctors, nurses, and the staff were for the most part, were very dedicated to healing the sick. They all deserved much more money than they were paid. To their credit, a lot of real good doctors took their internships there before going on to more lucrative private hospitals or private practice. And, to be fair, several good doctors came and donated time to the hospital. Also, they could be counted on in times of disaster (natural or manmade), or a special or unusual case.

Mr. North drove into the hospital parking lot and right up to the Emergency Room entrance. He was also impressed with the size of the hospital and the number of cars and people. This was not anything like the small county hospitals back in East Texas he was used to. He did feel that, as big as it was, it was a hospital for the common people. And from the looks of things, lots, and lots of common people.

"I believe it was Lincoln who said God must have loved the common people, because he made so many of them,"

Father quoted to Mother.

Mr. North only went to the ninth grade in high school before he left home to go to work, but he liked to read a lot. It was one of his greatest desires that his firstborn son finish high school and even go to college. From all his reading he would come out with quotes like this every so often, even if he did not always get it completely right or credit it to the correct author.

Mr. North got out of the car and carried his son into the hospital while Mrs. North slid over to go park the car. Orderlies took Adrian as Mr. North identified himself and Adrian. He explained that Dr. Hickory was supposed to have called ahead with information that they were coming. "Yes" they confirmed, "Adrian was expected." He was quickly and efficiently wheeled into an emergency examining room.

Mother hurried to Adrian's side while Father went

to fill out lots of admittance papers. Charity or not, insurance or not, there was always lots of papers to fill out and sign.

A nurse came in and told mother that she or mother must take <u>all</u> Adrian's clothes off...everything...and put them in a bag she had furnished and put on a hospital gown. Even as sick as he was, Adrian started to protest.

"Mother, do I have to take all my clothes off, even my underwear, right here in this public building," he exclaimed in horror. "And look at that thing. It looks like a dress and there is not even a back in it. The nurse said it tied in the back. It only has those strings to tie it together and I can't even reach them when I put it on to cover my front. And, Mother look. This room does not even have a real front wall, it is just a curtain hanging there. People are walking by, right on the other side!"

"Well yes, that is what people wear when they go into hospitals. As far as a room, I am sure that they will give you your own room shortly. I am afraid you will experience many more things that you are not used to while you are here in this hospital," she said.

"I feel almost naked," he said in protest.

"I know, dear," Mother said. "But you will be all right. Besides, everyone else who stays in the hospital has to wear them also."

"Well, I don't like this hospital already," he stated. "How long do I have to stay here?"

"Not too, very long, I hope. Not very long," she said, not very convincingly.

Adrian could see his mother was about to be in tears, so he stopped complaining for a little while. He hated to see or make his mother cry.

Father returned and not very long afterwards, they did move Adrian to a room. As a precaution, they put him in a room in the contagious ward. His parents had to put on masks and wear gloves when they touched him.

His Mother wanted ever so much to take him in her arms and hug him. Adrian felt he would never be too big for his Mother to give him a big hug. In fact, hugging was something his family and his country relatives did a lot. He had seen big tough grown men like his dad gave each other bone crushing hugs when they met.

The rest of the day became a blur of activity in Adrian's room. The doctors kept coming and going. They kept giving him shots and taking blood samples. Adrian wondered if he was going to have enough blood left. They took him out for x-rays and more tests, and then even more tests. Every time Adrian thought they were going to leave him alone, here they would come again. Sometime, long after dark, they did finally stop coming. A nurse was assigned to look in on him every few minutes all throughout the night. Mother and Father went to the waiting room. They had called Aunt Stella May and asked her to watch the kids overnight and give them a hug and kiss good night for Mother and Father.

Soon the only sound in Adrian's room was the labored breathing of Adrian. He was so tired and had been interrupted so very many times that he did something he had not done since he could remember. Adrian forgot to say his prayers.

Chapter Six
Day 13: [Thur.] Polio Official

Very early the next morning, the doctors came into the waiting room and called Mr. and Mrs. North. They had spent a restless night trying to sleep in a couple of waiting room chairs made for sitting, not sleeping. These poor chairs had pulled that same duty many other nights. In fact, there were three other couples who had spent the night here as well. This waiting room was in the ward dedicated to children. Somewhere on the ward, a child had cried all night. The vending machines were out, and the cafeteria was not open yet. Everyone had to settle for water from a low-pressure water fountain.

A Doctor came up to the Norths and addressed them. "Will you come into our office please? Please have a seat. I am Dr. Billings Chief Pulmonologist, that means I specialize in respiratory diseases. This is my colleague, Dr. Jones. We have been studying your son's tests most of the night. We have some conflicting tests. In cases like this, we believe the parents should know as clearly as possible our findings. We have information for you that I am afraid is not good. From what we have been able to discover, your son does not have Diphtheria as the good Dr. Hickory suspected. What he does have is an entroviruse belonging to the piconaviridac family. This virus causes infantile paralysis or Poliomyelitis, commonly called Polio."

Both Mr. and Mrs. North gasped and Mother started to weep and say over and over, "Oh my poor baby, Oh my poor baby."

After a moment Dr. Jones continued, "We sincerely wish this could have been better news. Unfortunately, we do not know as much about the treatment of Polio at this time, as we would like. We do know that there seems to be three types, which we call Types 1,2, and 3. Type 1 is the most paralytogenic. That means it does the most damage. We have, as yet, to determine which type your son has. I don't want to give you false hope, but in many cases with Types 2 and 3 the patient recovers, albeit, often with complications such as paralysis. I know that you probably could care less about these statistics, but about 50% of infected individuals recover with little residual effects. About 25% of infected individuals have residual disabilities, and only 25% have severe permanent residual disabilities. It has been found that the recovery of muscle function can take from six months to six years."

"We have put Adrian in an isolation ward," continued Dr. Billings. "We are not sure how long he can be infectious. It could be a few days or up to six weeks. You can go in and see him in about 30 minutes. You will have to wear a mask, gloves, and a gown, which must be discarded in the proper container upon leaving his room. Also, we would like you to get a shot. Which, we can give you right here. We, as yet, as you may know, do not have a vaccine for Polio, but a great deal of research is being done. Many brilliant scientists are giving it their full attention. The shot we will give you is not a cure but should go a long way in preventing you from being infected."

Dr. Jones took up the narrative, "If you have other children I hope you have kept them out of contact with...looks at the form he is holding...Adrian. All the clothes he has worn in the last three to four days should be destroyed, preferably burned." All this was said in a matter-of-fact impersonal tone, as if the doctor was instructing a group of interns.

"We have kept the other children away from him as soon as we saw how sick he was," commented mother, a little offended. "Dr. Hickory told us about the clothes thing being a possibility." Mother said. She did not really care for his tone of voice no matter how smart he was.

It seemed they practiced this team instruction because Dr. Billings finished the instructions. "Again," he started, "Let us just say we wish we had better news. We are terribly sorry. A nurse will come out in a little while and take you to see him. She can supply you with the gloves, mask and gowns."

While these two doctors were very dedicated physicians. They spent all their energies and time studying. They were good at what they did. However, they tended to devote so much of their attention to studying illnesses and how to discover and administer the care thereof, that they overlooked one important thing: the human element. The principal reason for their effort was the human patient. People have feelings and emotions. They were not just cold hard facts. Being a really good doctor should include what was called, "a good bedside manner".

The doctors let the North's out of the office and hurried away, already discussing another patient. They did, however, stop by the nurse' station. Dr. Billings spoke to the Nurse. "Nurse Jennings, the County Board of Health must be notified of another confirmed case of Polio in the county this year. Will you see that it gets done?   It is the North child."

"Yes, doctor.," answered Nurse Jennings. She then lowered her voice and asked, "How bad is he?"

"We can only hope it is a type 2 or 3," he answered sadly.

When the North's entered Adrian's room a little later, his eyes lit up. He reached out to them to give them a hug.

"Oh, I am so sorry honey, but we cannot touch you just now," Mother said, amid tears, "We have not got our gloves, as yet. They just ran out."

"Alright, I don't like it, but I understand," Adrian mumbled. "Oh, Mother and Father I am so scared, and I feel so bad. Why is everybody wearing those funny looking blue gowns and weird masks? You all look like a bunch of bad guys in the movies." His words tumbled out like spilling a bag of beans, which he had done once.

Mother, trying to sound much more confident and comforting than she felt, answered, "I know that you feel really sick. All the doctors and nurses are trying to help you get well so you can go home again. Don't be scared. You will probably be out of here before you know it."

Father spoke up trying to divert Adrian's attention from how he felt and to answer his questions, "You have probably seen too many movies. Bad guys are not the only reason people wear masks. The doctors say that the sickness you have is very contagious. That means other people can get it from you real easy. You don't want to make other people sick, do you?"

"No way," Adrian exclaimed.

Father continued "As far as the blue gowns, the color is to identify what the gown is for. This gown is to let people know to keep away, so they don't get your germs on their clothes. Also, the mask keeps germs out of peoples nose and mouth. Also, if they have germs, it keeps their germs from getting on you."

"I have another question," Adrian said.

"You usually do, my little think box," father jokingly replied. Adrian was sharp beyond his years. He had an inquisitive mind and thus asked seemingly endless questions of everybody. His Father was glad about this, as he also wanted to know and learn everything he could. While he had a limited education, he did have an answer-seeking mind.

"Last night," Adrian began, "I was so tired that I forgot to say my prayers. Do you think God is mad or upset with me about that?"

"You do have some of the most interesting questions, young man. But to answer your question, I am sure God is not mad at you. While it is always good to remember to say your prayers, it is not some kind of law or rule. God understands things happen that we sometimes forget or, for some other reason, do not say our prayers. Of course, we don't want to make a habit of it. Son, God loves you more than you can ever know."

Then father did one of his quotes. "I don't know who said it but:

While we cannot always understand God's ways,
While we cannot always understand God's purpose
We can always trust God's heart.
We can know we will get God's best for us."

That satisfied Adrian, so he changed the subject to something else that was bothering him. "Last night I had to go to the bathroom really bad, so I pushed that buzzer thing like they told me to. Nurse Kincade came into the room. She said I could not get up out of my bed. She brought a bottle-like thing she called a urinal. She said boys could use it and then she put what she called a bedpan under me and said go ahead. Do you know how hard it is to go to the bathroom when you know someone is standing around waiting for you to? Well, I had to go so bad that I finally did my thing. And told her I was through. Then came the worst part of all. She came over, took the bedpan, rolled me over and wiped me just like you do baby Edmond, Mother."

Mother smiled and said, "I know that probably embarrassed you a lot, but you will find that will happen a lot here in the hospital. And Nurse Kincade was just doing her job. I am sure she did not think anything much about it. It is just one of the things a nurse has to do. There is nothing personal in it. She was probably not embarrassed at all, although I am sure she knew you were. She seems to be a caring, compassionate, and experienced nurse. She is used to such things."

"Well, she may be used to it, but I sure am not," Adrian retorted.

"You will be," Mother said sadly.

"Another thing Mother," Adrian lowering his voice and abruptly changed the subject said, "Why does Nurse Kincade smell so funny?"

"That smell is Lilac. A lot of ladies now wash with a soap that has that odor put into it. Actually, it is quite popular right now. It also comes in perfume. I don't care for it myself, but some women do." she explained.

"Well, I don't much care for it either, but I guess that does not matter," confessed Adrian.

About this time Nurse Kincade came into the room to tell Mother and Father in about 15 minutes they would have to leave the room. Visiting hours were over.

"You will come back and see me as soon as you can?" Adrian pleaded.

"You can count on it, son," Father replied. "You know we have the other children to look after and I have taken a lot of time off my job. You remember that I am trying to get enough money to get us into a nice real house."

Mother said, "We will come as much and as often as we can." She wished she could stay right there all the time, but she must think of the other children. She felt her heart was breaking.

Mother told Adrian that the hospital had strict visiting rules. Parents and immediate family could visit any day. Other visitors could only visit on Saturdays. The Candy Stripers could visit only during the week, not on weekends. Each Candy Striper chose one day a week to visit. One exception was clergy who could visit any day. All visiting was subject to hospital procedures, of course. No visitation was permitted if the patient was having a procedure done.

Nurse Jennings had called the County Board of Health as she was instructed and reported a new case of Polio. An alert reporter of The Houston Chronicle picked up the information. The article in the paper's early edition the next morning proclaimed the polio season was officially on the way. The third polio case for Harris County, 1946 was a small 9-year-old boy named Adrian P. North. He had been admitted to the County Hospital yesterday. It said that the hope was that polio had not spread to the boys two smaller brothers and one sister.

Adrian was sort of glad he could not get out of bed to say his prayers because even his knees hurt, and he did not think he could make it back into the bed anyway. He prayed as his cover prayer:

> *Lord Jesus I am really scared,*
> *I want to go home and I want to be well.*
> *Please, please, please help me to get better.*
> *Please bless my family a whole lot.*
> *Please help Nurse Kincade not to smell*
> *So strong of lilac soap.*
> *And don't let her stick me with needles so much.*
> *I guess I got to do the bedpan thing,*
> *So, please help me not think about it too much.*
> *Bless all the missionary kids,*

And heal all the sick people,
Especially in this big old hospital.

Please forgive me all my sins.
I truly am sorry,
It seems I just can't help myself.
I don't start out to be bad.
Then before I know it,
I say, do, or think something,
I know I should not do.
What is wrong with me Lord?
I am sorry I forgot to pray to you last night.
I did not forget you,
I just forgot to talk to you.
In Jesus' name, Amen

Chapter Seven
Day 20: [Thur.] Four Eyes

Adrian awoke when someone in the hall outside his room dropped a tray of something. It still took a second to remember where he was. Oh yeah, he was trapped in this hospital being stuck with needles every 30 minutes. Actually, that was not true. It was not near that often. But it sure seemed like it. It already seemed like he had been in this hospital for weeks and weeks.

Nurse Sally came in to do the "vitals". She looked sad. She sounded sad.

"What is the matter, Nurse Sally. You look like I feel," Adrian questioned.

"I am sorry Adrian. I did not get much sleep last night. My next-door neighbor has a new Hot Rod. He kept racing the motor most of the night. He says he is trying to increase the rpm's or something like that. I am not sure what really. But it has no mufflers or at least, very poor ones, I really don't know which but it just makes a terrible lot of loud noise. I really don't understand what he is doing, but I just wish he would do it somewhere else, or at least during the day. I am almost to the point of calling the police and reporting him for disturbing the peace. I learned that he just got back from serving in the Army. And I know he has had to see and do some terrible things. I know that he is a hero who gave a lot to protect our freedom. I appreciate our brave service men and am thankful for all they have done. However, I don't believe all that gives him the right to disturb the neighborhood all hours of the night when decent folks are trying to sleep."

That was the longest speech Adrian had ever heard Nurse Sally make in his presence. She was really uptight. She was so upset about her sleepless night that she laid the chart on the bed instead of hooking back on the hook provided on the end of the bed, as she usually did.

Adrian picked it up with his right hand and started trying to look at it. He was curious about all the stuff they were always writing on that chart. Not only did it not make a lot of sense, all those numbers, but he was shocked to discover that all the writing seemed blurred to him. He rubbed his eyes and looked again. He had been noticing that things had started to look funny to him the last couple of days.

"Nurse Sally, why is this chart all blurred? he questioned.

Nurse Sally immediately forgot about her sleepless night and concentrated on her patient. "What seems to be the problem, Adrian?" she asked.

"I was trying to read your chart and it seems all blurry. In fact, you seem a little blurry as well," Adrian spoke, with concern in his voice.

"It is just probably just the lighting or maybe you have been straining your eyes too much," she commented, however, not very convincingly. "I will notify the eye doctor and he will look in on you."

Nurse Sally quickly finished the chart, took care of

the overnight unmentionables, and left the room. She had quickly replaced one soiled sheet and a pillowcase.

Adrian was not too happy about being checked over by another doctor, but what could you do? Also, he was a little concerned about his eyes.

Later the orderlies came in and put him in a wheelchair and took him to a room on a different floor of the hospital. There was a strange little man with the brightest, reddest hair and the biggest ears Adrian had ever seen. Adrian had been taught not to stare at people who are different, but this fellow took all he could do to either laugh or be afraid of him.

This doctor was a highly respected eye doctor who gave two days a month to work at the charity hospital.

The first thing he did was have Adrian cover one eye and try to read letters on a paper chart thing on the wall, with letters that got smaller toward the bottom. It all looked blurred with both eyes, even the big letters. Next, the fellow shone a light in his eyes with his face only inches away, looking through some kind of lens thing into each eye.

The doctor's real name was Dr. Fred Carpenter. But Adrian decided to call him "**Red Ears**", but not to his face, of course. Red Ears had Adrian look at that paper thing again with a different lens on a kind of stick-like thing. He did them two at a time. Red Ears kept asking, "Is this better or is this?" They went through this about a thousand times, or so it seemed to Adrian. Finally, the doctor was satisfied.

He told the orderlies to take Adrian back to his room. Adrian was thinking that he got his naming things after his Mother. It was a country trait that she was steeped in. She had a name for everyone and everything. She called Adrian "Brother". She called Ann "Sister." She called her natural brother "Son." She had a name for each car, such as "Gray Boy," or "Big Red." Country folks liked two people names, such as "Billy Bob" or "Sallie Mae." Then there was the full name thing. If a country kid heard his full name, he knew he was usually in trouble.

In the country heart, to nickname something or someone was to make it or them seem either personal, or familiar, or companionable. Then again, many did it because it was just how they were raised.

What puzzled Adrian is the way some city folks call people by a completely different name than their real name. He knew a kid at one of the schools that everybody called Bob. Come to find out his real name on his school papers was Robert. Another kid was called Bill and his real name was William. That just did not make sense to Adrian.

Back in his room, Adrian slept awhile, then was awakened by a surprise. Dr. Carpenter came to see Adrian in his room. It seemed that Adrian's eye prescription exactly fit a pair of glasses that Dr. Carpenter had made for a child in the same hospital as Adrian was in. However, before the child could pick them up, he had died. They had already been paid for and if they fit Adrian's face, Dr. Carpenter could see no reason not to let Adrian have them free. They were very nice glasses. In fact, the frames were made of gold, not plastic or steel that would stain a kid's face and leave a mark if he were to sweat a lot. Adrian had seen kids with green rims on their glasses.

Low and behold, they fit like they had been made for Adrian. Adrian was very glad and very sad at the same time. First, he was happy to have such nice expensive glasses. Also, it appeared that he needed them, because he could definitely see better with them on. But at the same time, he did not like the idea of having to wear glasses at all. They were something a guy would have to keep up with all the time. He figured it would seriously limit him in the rough and tumble way he played, as he was figuring on getting well and getting out of this place.

They did come with a string-like thing that you could tie behind your head so that if they slipped off your face, they would not fall to the ground. They also came with a nice case. Dr. Carpenter (Adrian felt ashamed of calling him Red Ears) was very nice. He also included with the glasses a cleaning cloth and some nice glass cleaner to clean them with. He really was truly a nice man no matter what he looked like.

Besides all the hassle of having to keep up with wearing glasses, there was another drawback of wearing glasses. Adrian was sure he would be called "Four Eyes." Now that was a put down and unkind thing that he was ashamed to admit that he had called others. Father had told him that your sins will always find you out. The shoe was on the other foot and now he could already imagine how he would feel the first time someone called him that.

Father had mentioned that as much as he hated

Adrian being in the hospital, a side effect it was having was it was maturing Adrian. Adrian was learning some lessons taught by hard knocks. Father said trouble in life will teach you, one way or another. You can become better or bitter in your spirit. In fact, it is one of the ways God uses to teach us some lessons we would refuse or be unable to learn any other way. We can call on God to help us recognize sin and deal with it, or we can just live in the muck and mire of sin in our life. One of the troubles of the muck and mire of sin is, it really stinks. Soon everyone around you can smell it. The decision is up to you. You can get into trouble both on purpose or by just living in this sinful old world.

God does not set up traps of trouble. But he will save you and use whatever happens in your life for good if you let him.

Father also told Adrian that probably the best way to be prepared when trouble comes is to memorize scriptures. Then when troubles do come... AND they will and do come to everybody... you will know how to call on God for help.

Adrian realized that calling Dr. Carpenter, "Red Ears" was not funny or nice. Even if he only thought it to himself. Then he also realized his memories of calling people with glasses "Four Eyes" was also not funny and certainly not nice. It was so easy to get into sin. You need to stop and think before you say something that could be hurtful to others. He needed to ask God for forgiveness.

That night his prayers were;

Here I am again Lord
I have had a strange day

As you know.
Dear Jesus please forgive me,
For calling people hurtful names.
Please help me to never do it again.
I am also not too happy to have to were glasses
But you know best.
If it is in Your will
Will you fix it so I don't need them?
I believe you can heal my eyes,
While you heal everything else.
The Bible says you healed,
All kinds of stuff and diseases,
Like something called Leprosy.
Polio is probably just as bad.
Dr. Carpenter turned out,
To be a nice Doctor.
The glasses are really nice,
But I hope I don't have,
To continue to wear them long.
Please help me to be a better boy.
I just keep messing up.
Please bless Mother and Father,
And Lee and Ann and Edmond,
Ann all my other relatives.
You sure gave me a lot of them.
Thank you for everything.
Amen!

Child's Gold Rimmed Glasses from 1946

Chapter Eight
Day 22[Sat.] Aunt Lolla Bell

Adrian woke on Saturday to what looked to be a beautiful day outside. The Sun was shining, and it looked like a gentle breeze was blowing. He was not throwing up this morning. Actually, he felt better than he had in several days. That is not to say that he felt well, just better. He asked the nurse if she could open the window. She said she would open it just a little bit after she finished checking his blood pressure and all that other boring routine. After she had gone, Adrian daydreamed that if he were home, he and Lee would have probably dispatched a whole gang of bank robbers by now.

Then he heard her! "Where is my favorite nephew?" a female voice loudly proclaimed from his room's door. A wild sight came bursting into his room. That was the only way to describe Aunt Lolla Bell. She always dressed what mother charitably called "outlandish". Today she had on red bell-bottom pants, a bright yellow blouse, and some kind of flowery hat. Covering all that she had on the necessary gloves, mask, and blue gown. As bad as he felt Adrian had to start smiling.

She was carrying a large sack that she must have sneaked past Nurse Kincade doing the rounds. She was his first real visitor.

Aunt Lolla Bell was father's younger half-sister by

grandpa's third wife. Adrian had asked in the past how somebody could be half a person. Father said that it did not mean someone was some kind of half-person. What it stood far was, people who only had one parent the same and the other parent different. It still sounded really strange to Adrian but he was glad he was not somebody's half-someone.

Although Aunt Lolla Bell had gone to college for a while, she was all country. She still had some of the bark on. Maybe a lot, in fact.

Aunt Lolla said, "Guess what I have here?", but before he could he could answer with a guess, she began to take it out of the big sack. It turned out to be a Little Abner wind-up band toy. Little Abner was standing in front of a piano dancing up and down. Playing the piano was Abner's girlfriend, Daisy. On the left side was Little Abner's Pappy Yokum, playing a drum. And on the top of the piano was Mammy Yokum, leading the band with her corncob pipe and waving a baton. They were all hooked up somehow so that they all moved back and forth as the piano played. The piano did not actually play music, it only went through the motions. Aunt Lolla quickly turned the key in back and it started playing. It was fascinating. He had seen them in the stores but never in his wildest dreams thought he would actually have one.

But that was not all. There was something else in the sack. She pulled out a bright red plastic convertible wind up car. It was real pretty and what Father would call, "A real classy car like the rich people own."

Adrian was really impressed. "It is not Christmas or my birthday Aunt Lolla," Adrian stammered.

"Well, you are a special boy, and this is a special occasion, you being in the hospital and all," she said.

Adrian's busy mind kicked in and he said, "Aunt Lolla, you know how my mind goes from stuff to stuff. Father calls it going down, Bunny Trails"

Also, I like to tell stories about the exciting things that always seem to be happening to me."

"Yep! I am with you kid." she answered.

"Well, I really, really, like presents because they show special occasions and that people are special like you, and that they like you" he said.

She was not sure where he was going with this.

"I guess that I got my love for presents from Mother. My mother has "present-getting" with a passion. She told me that when she was a very little girl, her dad worked in the oilfields. While working on an oil derrick, a loose board fell out of the platform in the top of the derrick. Men yelled for her father to run. Instead of running, he looked up. The board hit him in the head and killed him. This was at Christmas time. In fact, presents had already been bought. The pretty little doll Mother got that Christmas was the last real present her mother ever gave her. Grandma was so upset at losing her husband at that time of the year that she never gave real presents to her children again, Christmas or birthdays. Even after she remarried. She would give them fruit or sometimes candy but no real presents."

Adrian's mother had, from an early age on, determined that no matter how poor she was when and if she had children, they were going to get real presents even if only one... both on birthdays and Christmas. She always made a big deal of those special days. Christmas always had to have a tree of some kind. A birthday was not a birthday unless you had cake and ice cream. Even if, on occasion, you had to celebrate it on the wrong day for some reason. Adrian had got his love of presents and celebrating from her.

Aunt Lolla wound up the Little Abner Band and let it run several times. Then she made a big mistake. She got the car on the floor to show how fast it could go. As it sped across the floor, who should come through the door but Nurse Kincade? The car banged into her foot.

"What in the world?" she uttered in surprise. "What do you mean by bringing these toys in here? Don't you know that they cannot be removed except by a very special cleaning?"

"I did not bring them here to have them removed or to take back home! I brought them here for Him!" Aunt Lolla said in her usual top of the lungs voice, pointing at Adrian.

Adrian was frozen in astonishment.

"That is another thing," Nurse Kincade said. "You must keep your voice down. This is a hospital, not a ball game."

"Okay! Okay! I will keep it down," Aunt Lolla replied, somewhat subdued.

"I thought she was going to throw you out of here," Adrian sputtered after Nurse Kincade left.

"Well, it would not have been the first time I had been tossed out of somewhere," she remarked.

Adrian thought he detected a bit of pride in that statement, although he could not understand why.

Aunt Lolla decided she wanted a cup of coffee. She was gone a while as the machines were on another floor. She came back and promptly spilled some on the blue gown. It was not a bad spill but it did seem to upset her somewhat.

She started a tirade about coffee. "Coffee," she began, "is one of life's little luxuries that most people or machines seldom get right. It seems that hospital vending machines are the worst. I was lucky but the poor man after me was not so lucky. This poor man put in three quarters trying to get one decent cup of coffee. The first cup came out no cream, but with sugar, and I watched him punch all the right buttons. The next cup came out with sugar but no cream. The third cup actually came out empty. But I think he handled it well. He took the first two cups and pored half of each into the empty cup and started drinking it. He said he was going to be there a while so he had time to drink a second cup of his really expensive coffee. You know, I hear they charge as much as a dollar a cup in some of those really, fancy restaurants."

Aunt Lolla added, "Also I had two friends in college that tried to make coffee. One made it so strong you could bend a spoon in it and the other made it so weak that it would not even stain a tablecloth if you split it."

Adrian said, "Mother says I should not drink coffee till I am grown. Both Mother and Father drink it, but she says it will stain me the color of the coffee if I drink it as a kid. She usually has a weird grin when she says that, so I think she is kidding and just does not want me to drink it."

"You obey your mother. Mothers know best," instructed Aunt Lolla.

Aunt Lolla stayed about an hour longer, then said she had better be "heading for the tall timber." This was her way of saying she was going home.

"I really am glad you came to see me, Aunt Lolla.," Adrian told her. "I don't get to see you very often anymore. And I just love the presents. You are the first real visitor I have had, and you brought presents as well. I believe that is really something special and exciting."

"Sure hon! You are special, I am special. And us special people got to stick together." was her remark.

"I will be back, The Good Lord willing and the creek don't rise." she spoke.

Then shortly, like a whirlwind or an east Texas twister, she sort of whirled out of the room, leaving perplexity and awe in her wake.

The rest of the day was pretty uneventful. He did have a spell of coughing that drained him of energy.

Adrian's cover other stuff prayer that night contained these lines,

> *Lord, please bless Aunt Lolla,*
> *She is kin and I know you care about her,*
> *You sure did not make all of us the same,*
> *And I don't know if I am like her as she says.*
> *But if I am let it be in good ways*
> *I just really pray I am like her in good ways.*

Please bless my family,
And all my kin folks.
Please heal me,
And everybody in this here hospital.
Please do it really quick, Jesus.
I really like the toys Aunt Lolla
Brought me today.
I want to play and enjoy them,
So, the sooner You make me well,
The sooner I can.
Help me be a good boy,
Cause I don't always
Seem to be able to do it on my own.
In Jesus name,
Amen.

Little Abner's Band Toy

Chapter Nine
Day 24: [Mon] Hospital Food and Updating Mother

Adrian had been the hospital for a little over a couple of weeks now. But it seemed to him, to have been weeks, and weeks, and weeks. His head hurt. He had a fever off and on. Some days, he vomited a lot. Actually, he felt bad all the time. He had started to think in terms of it not being not too bad a day when he could go all day without vomiting. His left side seemed to feel real week. Most, if not all, his muscles on his left side ached all the time.

On this early afternoon, the young nurse named Virginia, was trying to get him to eat his lunch. It had been delivered an hour ago by the kitchen staff and he had hardly touched it.

Sober looking but kind, Nurse Kincade came in. She told him he really needed to try to eat. She had taken a liking to him since that first night she had sat with him. She knew that, as a professional, that a nurse should not get attached to any one patient. However, the heart does not always listen to the brain. She had started to sometimes call him, "Little Trooper".

Adrian kind of liked her also, except for her smell. Although, either she had started to use less of that soap or else he had become more used to it.

"Now Adrian, you just got to eat something and be

a good Little Trooper," she coached. Sadly, they all knew that the chances were high that he would probably throw it up. The doctors were already trying to introduce more vitamins and minerals into his food.

Adrian did try a few bites but, really only just nibbled. He had lost his appetite. This from a kid who used to have to be shooed away from the table. He was finding it was starting to become hard to swallow. Between the vomiting and his sore throat, the muscles in his throat felt raw all the time.

"Say, Little Trooper, you really ought to eat your vegetables," said Nurse Kincade.

"I know! I know! That is what Mother always says. Only at home, the main vegetables we have are turnip greens, beans, and potatoes. My little sister calls beans and potatoes beenes and tazzes. My Father is trying to break her of it. Every time she wants potatoes, she has to say, Po-Ta-Toes. She is actually getting better at it except when she is in a hurry." protested Adrian.

"I don't know what some of this stuff is. How come this hospital does not serve simply beans and potatoes instead of things a good old country boy has never seen before? And when you do serve potatoes, you do things to them that I am sure Mother Nature never intended," Adrian said.

"Maybe you ought to try them then, you might like them," suggested Nurse Virginia.

"I figure that a fellow ought not to put anything in his mouth that he does not recognize and that has such strange smells," Adrian commented. This was his evaluation of his lunch.

"Well at least try the Jello, it is soft and sweet," Nurse Virginia pleaded.

"DON'T EVEN GO THERE," Adrian almost shouted. "You want to make me sicker than I am now?"

Nurse Virginia was taken back, "What did I say?"

"Never mind Virginia," said Nurse Kincade, who knew the story of the Jello.

"Please try your orange juice. You seem to like that," Nurse Kincade gently asked, as she and Nurse Virginia walked over to the door and began to talk.

Adrian could hear what they were saying because he had exceptionally good hearing. More than once, it had gotten him into trouble overhearing conversations not meant for his ears. So far, the polio had not affected his hearing in the least. It did seem sort of strange to him that here in the hospital the nurses and doctors did not act like grownups usually do. Usually, grownups try to talk really low when they are saying things, they do not want a kid to hear. Here they talked like the kid was not even in the room.

Nurse Kincade explained to Nurse Virginia, "He had a bad experience with Jello that caused him to really dislike it and it actually makes him sick."

"I didn't know," Nurse Virginia said apologetically.

"It is alright," Nurse Kincade said, in her most instructional tone as a head nurse. She went on to say, "You know, it is really sad. Here in this hospital, we get farm surplus and government welfare food money. Many of the kids we get in here have never tasted or seen some of the good and healthy foods we are able to give them. There ought to be some kind of program where kids who live in and around cities could at least get this food, even if on a limited basis.

You are a woman ahead of your time or at least out of step with it. Either way your heartfelt compassion shows. I gave Adrian some orange juice the other day and he said he had only tasted it twice before in his whole life. He said he thought only the rich folks drank Orange Juice. Can you imagine?" commented Nurse Virginia.

"That is really not exactly what I said," thought Adrian.

"Try to get some of it down him, if he really has taken a liking to it," instructed Nurse Kincade, as she exited the room to work her rounds.

Adrian really did like the orange juice. He sipped at the straw and pondered hospital food. He recalled, he definitely did not like bananas or watermelon. At one time he had liked them both but he had gotten sick on each of them in the past and now he could not stand them. What made something you loved turn into something you could not stand? You could also come to not even stand the flavor. He tried some watermelon-flavored gum one time, and he had to spit it out. Also, he had wasted his nickel. Was he weird or did this happen to other people? Maybe it happened in other things as well! He remembered thinking something like this can happen between married people, like when they got divorced. How could you love someone enough to marry them, then come to a place where you hated them?

Adrian decided he was thinking too hard about stuff he did not understand. He was going to have to ask

Father about this sometime. It was starting to make his head hurt.

To his great delight, Mother entered the room. Now this was someone who would never change and who always loved him. To him, she looked what he thought an angel would look like. She still had to wear the mask. The hospital now had a good supply of gloves

and gowns, with which she was appropriately clad. She came over and squeezed his arm.

"How is my Darling Baby Boy?" she asked.

"Mother, I am not a baby," Adrian corrected her.

"Oh, of course not. You are my big, brave, young man," she corrected herself.

"Well, I don't know how brave I am either, to be honest," Adrian confessed.

Adrian decided to change the subject. "Mother look at the neat toys I have gotten. Aunt Lolla brought them Saturday. They are under that sheet."

Mother took out the Little Abner's Band, "I have seen these in the stores. They are really nice and expensive. I would have liked to buy one of these for one of you my children." She wound it up and let it run a couple of times.

Next, Mother took out the red convertible. "This is really nice as well," said Mother. She held it in her hand and let the wheels turn.

"The wheels turn fast, I bet it really goes." she commented.

"It does, but don't try it on the floor," Adrian cautioned. "Aunt Lolla did that and got into all kinds of trouble with Nurse Kincade. She ran over Nurse Kincade's foot with it."

"She did what?" Mother questioned.

Adrian related the events of Saturday and the **Great Car Race**, as he described it.

"I was shocked at what Aunt Lolla said, and I was scared for her, for yelling at Nurse Kincade," Adrian confessed.

Nurse Kincade also scolded Aunt Lolla for her loud talking. Only then, did Aunt Lolla calm down. Then, so did Nurse Kincade.

He told Mother that Nurse Kincade had ordered, in her most official sounding voice, that Aunt Lolla was to put the toys on the table and cover them with a sheet which she would find in that closet. Also, she was to keep her voice down.

"I heard her say as she left the room that the kids were supposed to be the ones in the beds. Adults should know that this was a hospital not a playground and certainly not a racetrack. That is the most excitement I have had since I had to come in here." voiced Adrian.

After a moment or two he went on, "Aunt Lolla said I was her favorite nephew and would always be her oldest nephew regardless of what could or might happen. I am not sure what she meant by all that. When she looked up, she looked like she was going to cry."

Then, turning to Mother, he made the statement, "Mother, they say if things keep going like they expect, the masks and gloves will not be needed after tomorrow. But there is one good thing that I am glad about those masks," Adrian said excitedly.

"What, pray tell, is that?" Mother asked.

"I think Aunt Lolla is really pretty and I like her a lot. Also, I am very glad she brought me such nice presents. But Mother you know what?" he asked.

"What?" she replied the second time.

Lowering his voice, he said, "I am glad you all still have to wear the masks."

"Why would you be glad about us still wearing the masks? I thought that you really, did not like them." Mother asked.

"Do you remember last year when we visited Aunt Lolla in Saratoga?" Adrian asked, lowering his voice, and looking somewhat serious.

Wondering what was coming next, Mother answered, "Yes. I remember, Why?"

"When we were leaving, and everybody was saying goodbye and hugging and all that mushy stuff, Aunt Lolla kissed me right on the mouth. Ugh! Nobody has ever kissed me right on the mouth. You don't even do that. I guess I don't mind a kiss on the cheek or on the top of my head like Grandma does, but on the mouth Ugh! That is the kind of kissing that only grownups do," Adrian looked, horrified.

"I bet that if she had not have had that mask on, she would have done it again," he remarked.

Mother tried not to laugh and said, "I understand, but it will not be too long that there will come a day that kissing on the mouth might not seem as bad to you as it does right now."

Adrian changed the subject again. "Mother, I really

do miss seeing Lee and Ann and Edmond. How are they all doing?"

"They are all fine and they miss you too. They keep asking when are you coming home?" She answered, somberly.

"I wish I could go home and see them right now. I also want to know when I will be able to go home. When am I going to get well, Mother?" Adrian had asked these same questions over and over again to the doctors, nurses, and anybody he could.

"Honey, we are all hoping and praying it will be real soon. We all want you to get well, get out of the hospital, and come home where you belong," she announced with more hope than she felt.

Mother straightened up the toys on the table and covered them back up with the sheet. She then gathered up her blue shawl and blue matching purse. "I have to go now, Son. Sorry I can't stay longer. I know you get lonely up here," Mother said, as she prepared to leave.

"You got that right, Mother. There are plenty of people around here, but all they want to do is feed you something you can't eat, or stick needles into you," he complained. "" What I need are some down-home folks to **Chew the fat with**, as Uncle Elmer used to say."

Mother came over and patted him on the head and squeezed his arm, "Well, I will get back as soon and as often as I can," she promised, as she went out the door.

A few minutes later, here came his supper. He had always called the last meal of the day, supper. At the hospital they called it dinner. Maybe that was the reason he did not like it, 'cause they did not know what to call it.

But he guessed that was kind of stupid. He just did not like the food and all the time his throat hurt.

Adrian sort of nibbled at his food. He ate some, but not much. When they came to pick up his tray, they found he had drifted off to sleep. He twisted and turned and they figured he was having a dream. Which he was.

He dreamed he was running and playing in a big grassy field with really lovely wildflowers just everywhere. He was having a great time. He did not hurt anywhere. He was chasing a large yellow and black butterfly. It had fluttered over near some nice woods, when a large man stepped gently out from behind a tree. He looked as if he had been walking and just happened to turn a corner and step into sight.

Adrian though he ought to be scared, but somehow, he was not. The man was dressed all in white. Also, it seemed he had some sort of things that looked like wings, on his back. Adrian could not see them very well. The man was facing him, and he seemed to be nearly seven feet tall. It really was strange. "People aren't supposed to have wings," he thought.

"Hello, Adrian." the man said.

"Who are you? How do you know my name?" Adrian questioned. He thought he ought to be afraid of such a stranger, but he was not, somehow. This guy seemed really nice and friendly.

"Actually, I am your angel and I know all about you," the angel replied.

"I got an angel?" Adrian stammered.

"Sure, God sends Angels down to watch over each of His children." the angel said.

"Wait a minute, I thought all angels looked like little naked babies with bows and arrows in their hands. And all they ever did was fly around and shoot people," exclaimed Adrian.

"Well, I am sure you have seen a lot of pictures that look like that, especially on Valentine's Day and in the movies, but that is not what real angels look like. You know you cannot believe everything you see in the movies," the angel explained. "That is really not the way real angels look. That is just made-up stuff. You know, just like made up stuff for the movies. And I am sure your folk have taught you that a lot of the stuff you see in the movies is not real, no matter how real it looks as if it is."

"Oh, yeah, I know all about that. Like when the bad guy gets shot in a movie and then, in another movie, there he is again, sometimes even as a good guy. I am not a little kid you know," Adrian replied defensively.

"I know you are not," the Angel replied.

"Let me see if I can explain it. Actually, I am in a form or shape that humans can see and recognize. You would not be able to look at me if I showed up like I really look like," the angel explained.

"Huh?" remarked Adrian.

"Also, I guess I would look really silly with no clothes on while flying around shooting people with bows and arrows, don't you think?" the Angel asked.

"Boy, I'll say," said Adrian, as he started to laugh. The angel started to laugh also. After they had laughed a while, Adrian asked, "So, what do angels do?"

"Well, my main job is to worship the Creator. Also,

an important part of my job is to take messages to people from the Creator."

"Do you remember the stories in the Bible that your parents have read and told you about, like the Angel that came to Mary, and the one that came to Joseph."

"Right! now I remember," Adrian said, as his face started to light up.

"Who is the Creator? Is that God?" Adrian wanted to know. Smiling The Angel replied, "The Creator....."

"Wake up! Come on wake up, Little Trooper. Time for your shot," It was Nurse Kincade, shaking Adrian awake.

Adrian shook his head and looked around. He was back in that awful hospital bed. Nurse Kincade was trying to find a place on his arm to give him a shot.

"I guess we have to go for the bottom again," she said as she rolled him over. "I know this is embarrassing to you, but we are running out of places to shoot you."

"I have an idea. Quit giving me so many shots," Adrian suggested, hopefully.

"Sorry, Hun, I can't do that. Doctor's orders, you know," she said, with a chuckle.

Adrian did not see anything funny about the whole situation. He had learned to live with the idea that in a hospital a fellow's privacy and being embarrassed did not count for much to the doctors or the nurses. Bedpans and being undressed was just something a fellow had to put up with. He still did not like it at all. Most of the time he tried not to think about it, and part of the time he was just plain too sick to care.

"Man, I was having the neatest dream when you

shook me awake. I was dreaming about an angel," Adrian tried to tell Nurse Kincade.

"Sorry, Little Trooper. Maybe you can go back to sleep and dream it again," she suggested.

Adrian could tell by the way she talked that she was not really paying any attention at all to what he was saying. She was concentrating on her duties.

Adrian said to himself, "It really seemed real." This was not one of his usual dreams. Most of the time he dreamed about what he had been doing during the day. Also, a lot of the time his dreams did not make much sense. He would dream goofy things, like he was able to fly but only about four feet off the ground and he could not land when he stopped flying. What was with that?

Also, most of the time he knew the people in his dreams. Sometimes they all acted really weird. He also dreamed he was a really brave superhero cowboy that could ride any house, out fight and shoot any bad guy in town, and ride off into the sunset. He could not ever figure where he was riding off to or why it was sunset.

That night after his two memory prayers, he prayed:

Dear Jesus, that sure was a good dream,
I guess you know that already.
Well, I want to thank you for it.
Thank you again for the real neat toys,
That you had Aunt Lolla done bring me.
Can you help her to learn?
Not to always talk so loudly?
She says I am like her in her loudness,
Please don't let it be so.
Please bless my family. Amen!

Chapter Ten
Day 27: [Thurs.] Meeting Polly

It was what Adrian had come to call "the strip everything day". He had learned that in this ward, about every so often, a whole gang of nurses and housekeepers descended on his room and did a top to bottom cleaning. It is true that they changed his sheet every day sometime during the morning, but this was different. They rolled in this rolling bed they called a gurney. They dumped him on it. (Actually, they were very gentle, but he termed it "being dumped"). Then they took out anything cloth and replaced it. The part he really disliked was with all those women in his room. They took down the curtains that shielded him from the hall and usually left the door open so anyone going up and down the hall could look right in. They even changed the sheet covering the toys. Of course, the took his gown and he felt they were not near quick enough replacing it. They took some kind of disinfectant and rubbed down all surfaces that might be handled, like doorknobs, his bed, and such. "Why, he might as well be naked in a parking lot," he thought.

After they put him back in bed and left, he began to reflect. He realized that they were only doing their job to keep the room sanitary. He was grateful that yesterday the order to stop wearing the masks and those blue gowns in his room had been given. These ladies were only looking out for his health. He was grateful that it was over, at least for a while.

The weather outside seemed to be a fair day. Only

partly cloudy. One of the ladies had remarked that the forecast on the radio had called for widely scattered showers later in the day. Adrian had heard another of the ladies' remark that was the way forecasters protected their jobs. If it rained anywhere in a fifty-mile radius, and one cloud was in the sky, the forecast was right. Adrian recalled that rain had played a big part in his being in this place. "It had been fun though, except for the fall," he shamefully recalled.

He had learned that the Candy Striper that was to visit him was due today. "What would she be like? "he wondered" He soon found out.

This pretty, young woman came into his room. She was smiling and seemed to bring a brightness to the room. And, yes, her outfit did have red and white strips on it. Mother had seen Candy stripers in the halls and had told him that the stripes were on something called a pinafore that they wore over their street clothes for two reasons. First, they identified them and second, they protected their street clothes.

She went across to his chart and looked up his name. "So, Mr. Adrian, how are we today?" she asked.

"I don't know how you are, but I am sick, and in the hospital," retorted Adrian.

"Okay, I see you have not lost your sense of humor in here," Polly replied. "Well, my name is Polly. Sometimes they call me Jolly Polly, but I don't really like that name. I am what they call here in the hospital a Candy Striper. I like to bring jokes to the patients to maybe cheer them up. Some grownups say they are dumb jokes but most of the kids like them. Want to hear today's jokes?"

"Sure. Why not?" Adrian replied, not knowing what to expect.

"Well, here we go," Polly started. "I decided that I would do chicken jokes for you today."

Why did the chicken cross the road?
Adrian, "Why?"
To see what was on the other side.

"I agree with the adults, that's not very funny." Adrian said.

Why did the Duck cross the road?
"Oh brother, another one."
Because it was the chicken's day off.

"That is a little better**,**" he said.

What do you call a chicken that
Crossed the road,
Rolled in the dirt, over and over,
Then recrossed the road?
"What?"
A dirty double crosser!

"Ha. Ha, now that was funny." Adrian laughed.

"Well, they have to grow on you." Polly commented.

"With that I have to agree. So, who are you really and why do you do this?" Adrian wanted to know.

"Well, I am Polly Goldsmith. My parents were missionaries. While I was still young, my dad died on the mission field. My mom felt called to work with children. She worked a while in the states with a group that did children camps, then started doing them on her own. She took us, her four children, with her and we learned to be part of the ministry she did. I am going to go to college as soon as I earn enough money. On my job, I have Thursdays off. So, I come to the hospital and work as a Candy Striper."

"One of my father's favorite scriptures was, *A merry heart doeth good like a medicine.* I tell and bring jokes and such, as a type of medicine to children in the hospital. I like children and I especially like to help children in the hospital whose life is really rough." Polly explained.

"That is what country folks call, **With The Bark On.**" Adrian said. "I guess I use that expression a lot".

"What does it mean?" Polly inquired.

"Well, it is like this, it is a country expression. My family uses it quite a bit. When you are talking about things, it kind of means real rough or hard on the outside. When you are talking about people it usually means they are rough or loud in manner or appearance, or just not city normal. My Father once used three big words to explain rough, usually country folks. He said they were not compatible, or conformable, or conventional, like most city folks."

You know what? Adrian said sort of thinking out loud, "my having Polio is sort of my life with the bark on."

"A country expression then. Where do you think it came from?" Polly inquired.

Father said, "It probably started back when folks had to build log cabins to live in. They did not have are could not afford manufactured building material. You see the logs have to lay on top of each other. Folks had to smooth two opposite sides as much as possible so there would be few cracks between the logs. It was extra work to peel off the bark on the other two sides so they usually left the bark on. Later the cracks could be filled with mud or a mixture of mud and straw. The outside looked sort of rough, but what you wanted was to get something up to live in as soon as possible. So, folks said it was a house with the bark on. Often the woman of the house would, later, when she had time and if they were going to live in the cabin a long while, would peel the bark off on the inside to make it look nicer for a longer time. Also, the peeled bark could be used as fuel."

"My father built a log cabin. It was his first house he lived in that he owned. He built it for himself and my mother to live in when they got married. She helped him build it. In fact, me and my brother were born in that one room log cabin. I bet not a lot of folks in this city can say that."

"You know what," Adrian said sort of thinking out loud, "My having Polio is sort of my life with the bark on."

My mother has an interesting story that happened while the lived in that log cabin. She was a young wife, not real experienced in cooking. She made some biscuits on the wood stove. She left them cooking too long, and they burned. She said, they were hard as rocks. She did not want Father to find out, so she took them out in the back of the cabin and buried them. Can you imagine that? She actually dug a hole and buried biscuits in the ground. Then she aired out the cabin, and cooked some more. She said it was several years before she shared that story to father. I think it is a fascinating story.

"That reminds me of something else. Stuff reminds me of stuff. Mother says I am always changing the subject. But really this story is about bark," Adrian eagerly said.

"My Father's birth Mother had lots of kin. They were the Martinsons. Aunt Margaret lives with Aunt Mary Lee and her husband. His name is Bartholomew Jones. They have on their property an old pecan orchard. It does not make enough pecans to sell any more. But to me, there still seems to be a lot. We love to go visit those two old Aunts. We kids love to visit in the fall when the pecans get ripe. We go out into the orchard and pick-up pecans off the ground. My little sister cried the first time she went out with us because all she saw was some ugly nut-like things laying on the ground. I told her, "Don't cry. The Pecans are inside that ugly shell or bark. I peeled it off for her and showed her the pecan, like you see in the store. Pecans were ugly with the bark on, but you peel of the bark and the good stuff is on the inside." Adrian explained.

"Did you know that pecans have an ugly outer bark?" Adrian asked Polly.

"Actually, I did not," confessed Polly.

"Also, Uncle Bartholomew is a salesman for the

Curtis candy company. He usually has lots of candy bars around the house and gives some to us kids when we visit. I like that almost as much as the pecans."

"A lot of my country kin folks are like that. You just have to look past the bark and get to know them." Adrian continued.

"You know, I meet a lot of folks on the mission field you might say have the bark on, as you call it," remarked Polly.

"Look under that sheet over there. Those are some great toys one of my kinfolks brought me. Her name is Aunt Lolla. Her having the bark on got her in trouble with Nurse Kincade. She talks really loud and she ran over Nurse Kincade's foot with that car. Nurse Kincade scolded her and told her to put the toys on the table and cover them with a sheet."

Polly made an observation. She said, "They are really neat toys, but they are kind of impractical for you right now. With you in the bed all the time, you can hardly play with them. You cannot even wind them up unless someone brings them over to you and then, afterwards, puts them back for you."

"I thought the same thing, but I did not want to say anything," Adrian confessed.

Adrian's mine took off down a bunny trail as he said, "That reminds me of some presents that my father's older half-sister and half-brother who lived up in Dallas gave me. Aunt Dorothy gave me a cuticle set. She explained the tools in it. It had two pair of scissors, a file, and four tools you were supposed to push that skin back that grows at the start of your fingernails and toenails and a nail file. It was really nice in a black leather case that zipped up with a neat zipper. Nonetheless, I fingered that was more for a girl than a boy. I have used the nail file and one of the scissors, a few times, but my nails don't get too long before I break them off. I still have it at home in my sock drawer. She also gave one to Lee, but I think he has already lost his," Adrian said.

He continued, "Uncle Douglas gave me an old cigar box with some old stamps in it. They were real interesting looking. He said I should save them and even collect more. He said that they might be worth a lot of money someday. I still got them also, but they are not a present you can play with or wear or something.

"Don't be discouraged. While it is true you don't see much use for them now, someday you may look back on these presents and appreciate them a lot more than you do right now," Polly said, trying to comfort Adrian. "Also, they are something personal you can remember your aunt and uncle by."

"I supposed you are right," he sort of begrudgingly answered.

You know the first time we went up to meet them, I got to work with my Uncle Douglas. I will never forget it. He was a rural newspaper delivery man. He had a route out in the country delivering the Dallas Morning News. He told the boy that regularly helped him to take the night off, because he had a nephew that was going to ride shotgun with him. I liked that cowboy talk but had no idea what I was about to get into. I had never done anything like that and was kind of scared. I sat in the back seat with a great big stack of newspapers. It was the

Sunday paper, with comics, circulars, and I don't know what all. He rolled a few to have some to work with and show me how. And we took off, him driving down country roads, stopping to poke them into newspaper holders at the end of driveways, and me rolling them as fast as I could. Boy, what a night! About 4 am, he pulled over and told me he had to nap a little bit. He gave me his watch and told me to wake him in about 50 minutes.

There I was in the middle of nowhere, somewhere way out in the country, in the middle of the night, with an uncle I had just met a few hours before. I tell you; I was somewhere between excited and scarred half to death. We made the rest of the night and got home in time for breakfast and the bed for me. I did overhear him tell my father that he had not expected it, but that was the biggest Sunday paper he had delivered in quite a while. He also told my Father that I had done a really good job. I tell you that made me proud. I was sleepy but proud.

Sadly, shortly after our visit, one morning Uncle Douglas had finished making his route, dropped off his helper, and was headed home alone when something real bad happened. Uncle Douglas was driving under a railroad overpass when a little girl ran out into the road right in front of him. He quickly turned the wheel to keep from running over the little girl and ran head on into the concert overpass. He sadly was killed, but the little girl was saved. I cried when I heard. I think my uncle was a real live hero, although I really hardly knew him.

Polly said that was quite a story. She said she though Uncle Douglas was a hero also. Then she said she had enjoyed visiting with Adrian and hearing his stories, but it was about time for her to go. She would like to drop in to see him next week if that was okay.

"You bet, I know I talk too much and bore you with all my stories" Adrian enthusiastically replied. "But I will be really looking forward to seeing you."

It was kind of a letdown after Polly left. After all the excitement of talking to her and telling those stories he had not had time to think how really bad he felt. It had gotten his mind off the sickness and the hospital routine.

What was that scripture Polly quoted? "A merry heart doeth good like a medicine'. I like that and I believe it is good medicine," Adrian said.

Adrian's third prayer went like this that night:

Dear Lord Jesus I do love You.
I thank you for all you do for me.
Thank you for sending this nice Polly Lady.
I am glad she took time to talk with me.
Please comfort Aunt Dorothy
Cause she ain't got Uncle Douglas no more.
Please bless Father and Mother,
And Lee, Ann, and baby Edmond.
Help all the sick people in this hospital.
Make us all well real soon please.
Could I have a good night's sleep?
Also, maybe a real good dream of angels.
Please forgive me the lots of times,
When I am bad and sin.
You know, Jesus, I really don't mean to.
Thank you that, with all you have to do,

*You always have time to hear my prayers.
Amen and Good Night.*

Candy Stripers

One Room Log Cabin

Chapter Eleven
Day 29: [Sat.] Biggest Liar In East Texas

On this day, when Adrian woke, it promised to be a really bummer of a day. It was raining and cloudy outside again. The gloom seemed to reach right into the room. Adrian felt lousy. The peace he had felt previously had turned to melancholy. Would this pain never end? Was the old hospital routine of endless shots and bedpans and checking temperature and pulse never going to let up? The same old painful thing day after day after day. Both Nurse Kincade and Nurse Sally had the day off so a different and grumpy head nurse was in charge. This day, even the floor nurses who usually tried to act cheerful and friendly, seemed to be down in the dumps. It could be the different head nurse. Nurse Kincade was really strict with procedures and duties, but she was pleasant, both to patients and nurses alike.

Adrian had heard a couple of the nurses' snap at each other. Some girl down the hall had seemed to whimper all night. "I guess I am not the only one in a lot of pain," Adrian thought. Two nurses came into his room for the daily sheet change. They were talking about the kid one hall over. It seemed he was always complaining, and crying, and whining. The fact that his parents were the very wealthy and demanding kind, who wanted everything done for their little darling son immediately, did not set to well with the nurses. "I know he is sick and in pain, but so are all the other kids in here," one of them said.

The two nurses went over by the door and started talking. They started talking about their boyfriends. For once, Adrian wished he did not have such good hearing. Some of the things they talked about, he was sure he should not be hearing. One said they were glad it was Saturday. That gave Adrian had a ray of hope. Maybe someone would come today and brighten up his day. He tried to concentrate on listening to the rain. Finally, they left for a while.

Would he never be able to get up and run and play again? He thought how great it would be to be able to get up. Just to climb a fence or a tree or something would be great.

Adrian felt a wave of nausea pass over him. His head seemed to swim, and he was lying flat in bed. When it had passed, he wished he had a ball in here. At least he could hold it and roll it around the bed, or something. He realized he was really bored. He loved balls and playing with them. He loved to kick them, throw them, and hit them with a bat or anything else you could do with a ball.

Thinking of balls made him remember the time when he went to a certain city school for a short time. The guys were playing baseball, and someone hit the baseball over the chain link fence which went all the way around the school. There was a gate that was open, but it was a long distance away. If they had to go all the way down to the gate, then walk all the way back, to pick up the ball. It would take time. After throwing the ball back over the fence, that person still had to walk back to the gate and then back to the game. By that time, the recess would be over or nearly over.

Adrian had an idea. If a couple of the guys would hold up the fence on each side of him...it was loose on the bottom...he believed he could crawl under, get the ball throw it over, and crawl back under the fence. Even at that time he was kind of skinny. Then the game could go on in no time at all. A couple of the fellows agreed. Adrian went under the fence, threw the ball back over, and started back under the fence. While Adrian was only partially back under the fence, the two guys holding the fence saw a teacher coming. They turned the fence loose and ran. Adrian was pinned to the ground. He could neither go backward or forward. Not only was Adrian caught crawling under the fence, but he had taken his shoes off again and was playing barefoot, which was a second "no no". He was sent to the principal's office for two offenses. He took his punishment and never told on the other two guys. However, Adrian never trusted or liked those two boys very much after that.

It was still raining, and Adrian was hoping that since it was Saturday, someone would get out in the bad weather and come to see him. He sure wished someone would come in and brighten his day. About mid-morning, he got a big surprise. Into his room walked another of his uncles. Father said Adrian had more Uncles and Aunts than you could shake a stick at. Adrian could not figure what the shaking a stick had to do with anything, but his folks said it a lot. "I guess it means many, 'cause I sure have a lot," he reasoned.

Into his room, walked Uncle Elmer Adrian Rodchester. He had been named after this uncle. Everybody said Uncle Elmer was a real character. He was a legend in the Big Piney Woods of East Texas." Adrian's father said, "There was not a man around here I would druther have if I needed help or anything. But that being said, he is the biggest liar in eight counties. You have to take everything he says with a grain of salt. He can stretch a simple happening into the most gosh awful yarn you ever heard, and swear it was the gospel truth. He is a real old curly wolf that still has the bark on."

Uncle Elmer boasted he was the best Hog Caller in the whole state of Texas 'cause he had such a big booming voice. Adrian was glad Nurse Kincade was not working today.

Whatever he was, he was a favorite of Adrian. He had never expected a visit from him because Uncle Elmer seldom left the piney woods. But he sure was here today. If the doctor had ordered something to cheer Adrian up, this sure would have been the right medicine.

"Howdy boy." boomed Uncle Elmer. "How is my namesake today?"

"As well as can be expected, I guess," Adrian replied.

"I see you got one of those IV things," observed Uncle Elmer. "I don't like those things. They really get under my skin."

Adrian smiled at the bad joke. Then he said "I am feeling kind of down in the dumps today Uncle Elmer, but I am really glad to see you."

"I know just what you mean boy. I am feeling down in the mouth myself," Uncle Elmer looked like he had lost his last friend.

Adrian should have seen it coming, but he bit and asked, "What is the matter Uncle Elmer?"

"Well you see, it's my old hound dog. You remember Old Blue, don't you boy?" Uncle Elmer asked with a straight face.

"Oh Yeah! What is the matter with Old Blue?" Adrian asked with concern.

"You see boy, it was like this. I was out in the yard the other day, and I was washing the grease off some car parts from my old jalopy with gasoline. I had the gasoline in an old coffee can on the grass. Old Blue came over sniffing, and first thing I know is that fool dog up and drank some of that gasoline. Well now, he ups and takes off around the yard as fast as he could go, as if he was chasing a coon and howling like he had a rear end full of buckshot. He makes about four trips around the yard. Then he stops all of a sudden, and falls over on his side, with his four legs sticking straight out, stiff as a board."

Wide-eyed Adrian asked, "Was he dead?"

"Naw! He just ran out of gas," Uncle Elmer said with a big grin.

"Uncle Elmer! You were just pulling my leg," Adrian said, laughing. He was starting to feel better already.

"Now boy, you don't think your Old Uncle Elmer would stretch the truth a mite, do you?" Uncle looked slightly offended. But Adrian saw the twinkle in his eye.

"Oh no! Not you!" said Adrian, getting into the spirit of the conversation. When you talked to Uncle Elmer, it was best to just go along with him, but don't believe a thing he told you.

"Just let me tell you about that thar daughter of mine, Velma May she acts real kinda dumb sometimes. Like when I dun told her and told her not to drive that old wreck of a car she has too fast. One of these days she was going to have trouble. The other day, she finally got into trouble, but as luck would have it, she got out of it herself," Uncle Elmer said, with what seemed to be a puzzled look on his face.

"What ever happened?" Adrian went along.

"Well, let me tell you. She was speeding down the highway lickety split, with all the windows down. Her blond hair was just a blowing everywhere. She claimed her long blond hair got in the way of her speedometer, but I don't believe it. Any way this blond-haired lady cop dun pulled her over."

"Let me see your driver's license," she demanded. "You were doing 57 in a 37-mile zone," she said.

"Velma May was all flustered and started looking in her purse for her driver's license."

"It's got your picture on it," the officer said, in frustration.

Velma Mae felt in purse and found the mirror she carried. It was the right size and when she took it out and looked, sure enough there was her face, plain as could be. So, she handed it to the blond lady officer.

The lady officer took one look at it and said, "Goodness. I did not know you were an officer. Look, because you are a fellow officer, I am going to let you off this time, but from now on I expect to see you observe the speed limit."

"Velma May took back her mirror, dropped it into her purse, and thanking the officer drove off," finished Uncle Elmer.

"Uncle Elmer, that is one of those dumb blond jokes that are going around," Adrian said laughing, in spite of himself.

"Not so," protested Uncle Elmer, "I just got some dumb young uns."

"Now you take that boy of mine, Chester. You remember Chester, don't you?" he asked.

Adrian, smiling and not knowing what was coming up next, answered, "Yes Sir, I remember Chester." Uncle Elmer did have a son named Chester.

"Now when Chester tells you something, you kind of wonder if he is playing with a full deck. Like last winter, for example, when he went up north to New York state near the great lakes, for a spell. Got him a job up thar. You did know he went up to New York, did you not?" Uncle said with fake concern.

"No Sir, I did not know that," Adrian answered, trying to keep a straight face. He knew Uncle Elmer was trying to draw him in, but could not help himself, without breaking the spirit of the story.

"Well, he did. Anyway, it seems there came up one of them big mean old snowstorms while he was out shopping at Montgomery Wards. He had been in the store for a spell. When he comes out the snow was blowing something fierce. It was blowing so bad he said you could hardly see six feet in front of you. Don't get them snowstorms like that up in the piney woods. Anyway, he remembered I had done told him that if he should get caught out in a blinding snowstorm like that, a good thing to do was try to get behind one of those big old snowplow trucks and follow them. They push the snow out of the way, and you can always see their tail lights ahead of you." Uncle Elmer said, as he was warming up to his story.

He had Adrian's attention. In fact, some more of the hospital help had heard his loud voice and were standing in the door listening.

"So, Chester, he sits there and sure enough along comes a big snowplow truck. He is happier than a pig in a new hog wallow. He pulls right in behind that truck and starts to follow. It works like a charm. It seemed the plow made a lot of corners, but he drove slow and Chester never lost sight of him. After about an hour and a half, the snowplow stopped, and the driver came back to Chester's car. Chester rolled down the window to see what he wanted." Uncle Elmer paused for a breath.

The plow driver says, "Excuse me sir, but I have noticed you back here following me for quite a while now. Is everything all right?"

Chester says, "Could not be better. My Pa done told me that if I am ever in a terrible snowstorm like this one, when I came up here, to get behind a snowplow truck and it would clear the road for me, no problem. It is working just great."

The driver shook his head and said, "I see! Well, you might want to know that I am finished plowing this

Montgomery Ward's parking lot, and I am headed down the street to do the Sears lot."

When Adrian could get his breath from laughing, he said, "Uncle Elmer, I don't believe that any body is that dumb, even Chester."

"His brother Floyd might run him a close second," said Uncle Elmer, with a straight face.

The two nurses who had been there earlier had come back into Adrian's room and were cracking up. There were about four of them now. Some would leave then come back. They thought they had never heard such yarns in all their lives. One thing about Uncle Elmer he loved an audience.

"What about Cousin Floyd?" asked Adrian. He knew another whopper was coming.

"Well, it seems that Chester had called and asked Floyd to mail him his big heavy winter coat up there to New York. You know the one with the big heavy brass buttons, and a big brass belt buckle with the shape of a pig on it. It's the one Chester won at the pig wrestling contest a couple of years ago." questioned Uncle Elmer.

"No Sir, I don't remember that," Adrian answered.

"Oh yeah! Quite a show it was too," bragged Uncle Elmer.

"Anyway, Floyd went in to ask the lady at the post office how best to ship it and how much it cost. She told him it was simple. Just put it in a cardboard box the size to fit the coat and be sure to tape it down really good. If it had no chemicals or breakables, then that was all he had to do. As far as the price, it would be charged by weight. She would, however, need to check the contents before he sealed it shut, sort of a government requirement."

"So, Floyd thinks he will outsmart the post office people. They are government folks you know. He gets out his pocket knife and cuts off all those heavy brass buttons and puts them in the inside coat pockets, along with that heavy old brass buckle. Now he figures since the lady can't see them, the coat ought to ship a lot cheaper."

"He didn't?" Adrian asked laughing.

"Yep! He shore did! and bragged how he had outsmarted the post office lady," was the reply.

"You know, my boys aren't too big on muscle power said Uncle Elmer, with a look of pretended sadness on his face.

Adrian could sense that this was leading into another story.

"Now you take my brother, Big Bubba," Uncle Elmer said, with a straight face.

"What about Big Bubba?" Adrian responded, playing along. He was really enjoying this, as were the hospital staff who were gathered just inside the door. Their number seemed to Adrian to fluctuate up to six, from time to time when he took time to look.

"Well now, I tell you," Uncle said, warming up. "He is a really big man. Lots of muscles, but real gentle and kind. But, you don't want to get a big man like that railed up. Our maw used to call him her *Gentle Giant*."

"Bubba went over to visit a neighbor to see some new coon and hog dogs the fellow had bought. The fellow had three good-looking coon dogs inside the front yard that they were looking at. The fellow said he had a hog dog penned up out back because the dog was so mean that he would attack anything. The fellow said he was going to have to figure how to tame the dog down some so he could handle him because the dog was so mean he would attack anything or anybody. He figured that would take considerable doing."

"The dog out back was barking and growling something fierce. He keep jumping up on the wood fence trying to get out. Finally, the dog made it over the fence and charged straight at Big Bubba. The dog made a great leap right towards Big Bubba's face." Uncle Elmer paused for effect.

"Did the dog bite him?" Adrian asked breathlessly.

"Well, no! Big Bubba reached out with tat big hand of his and grabbed that dog around the neck and squeezed. The dog whimpered a couple of times. When Big Bubba released him, the dog fell dead to the ground," Said Uncle Elmer, with a look of pretended sadness on his face.

"Wow!" was all Adrian could say.

"But that's not all to the story," continued Uncle Elmer. "That neighbor started in on Big Bubba about killing his new dog, which he had just bought. He said he had spent a lot of good hard-earned money on that dog."

"Big Bubba apologized to the man for killing the dog, he told the neighbor how sorry he was. Big Bubba said he would give the man the money he had spent on the dog. The neighbor would not stop carrying on about his loss. He went on and on about how he needed that dog, and how he had wanted a fierce dog that would also chase wild hogs off his property. He began to rag on Big

Bubba about how careless he was with other people's property."

"Big Bubba apologized again and again, and said he would replace the dog. The neighbor, however, went on and on, and began to get in Big Bubba's face and make threatening remarks."

""Finally, Big Bubba took all he was going to from the neighbor, and said again, "I told you I was sorry and I would replace your dog, but if you don't shut up about it and get out of my face, you could wind up like your dog.""

"The neighbor shut up, turned around, and walked into his house. He realized how close he had come to angering a really big and dangerous man. He and Big Bubba were not very close friends after that. Big Bubba did pay for the dog with a little extra."

"Wow, what a story," was all Adrian could say.

But Uncle Elmer was not finished. "I told you about Big Bubba in order to bring up Billy Bob, his son. My nephew is not over loaded with smarts any more than my boys. He inherited big muscles and frame from his dad, but not his gentle nature. Billy Bob is always getting into fights. He bragged to the crowd he ran around with, that he was **Bull Of The Woods** and **Meaner Than A Junk Yard Dog.** He had taken on every would-be challenger in his neck of the woods and beaten them all."

"One day his crowd of, hangers-on, got word that there was a guy down near Beaumont that claimed the title of **Bull Of The Woods.** They started in on Billy Bob to go down and check him out. Big Bubba heard of it and advised Billy Bob to leave it along. That only had the opposite effect. He decided he just had to defend his reputation and place in the eyes of those he ran with."

"Together with a few of his crowd he went to the bar on the outskirts of Beaumont where this fellow was said to hang out. Billy Bob strode into the bar like he owned the place. One of his buddies asked the bartender who it was that <u>claimed</u> to be **Bull of The Woods**. The bartender pointed out a big man sitting with a couple of men across the room. Billy Bob's buddy pointed him out to Billy Bob."

Billy Bob strode up to the fellow and said, "What's this that you think you can <u>claim</u> to be The **Bull Of The Woods**."

"Without saying a word, the big man stood up and hit Billy Bob so hard that he went staggering backwards across the room and wound up under a table.

Billy Bob got up and crossed the room once again. Again, the big man hit him and once again he wound up under the table.

Taking much longer, Billy Bob crawled out and said, "I'm still a come'n." He either bravely or foolishly headed back across the room where the big fellow was still standing. For the third time he was hit and knocked Billy Bob across the room and under the table.

Billy Bob's buddy went over to him and said, "stay under the table!" Billy Bob was heard from under the table through broken teeth say, "You know something, he is **Bull of the Woods**."

"What a yarn," Adrian thought.

"Well nephew, I guess I had better get my show on the road. I wanted to come see you, also your Aunt Molly

Ann said I should pick up some new boards and steel hinges. Besides, your Aunt Molly Ann says I get way to serious and all molly grubbed up when I visit a hospital. I need something important to keep my mind occupied," explained Uncle Elmer as he got up to leave."

If this was him serious, the Adrian though he could not stand it if he came in a jovial mood. Adrian knew he should not ask, but he could not pass it up. "Why do you need boards?" he ventured.

"Let me tell you, to fix the door on the outhouse," Uncle started to explain, as he sat back down. He said this with a dead serious face, as if it was the gospel truth.

"It was only yesterday afternoon about three o'clock. I had Old Blue chained to the outhouse door. It had a knot hole just the right size down near the bottom to run the chain through. Weren't no tree near enough to chain him up to. Well, this old 'he coon' ran across the south pasture, and Old Blue saw him. I think that coon was just ah taunting Old Blue. Old Blue started barking and jumping and pulling on that chain something fierce. That fool hound jerked so hard that he jerked that there door right off the outhouse. That has been a good solid door since my Pappy put it on there, years and years ago. The leather hinges weren't in too good of shape though. Old Blue lit in after that coon dragging the door behind him."

"Old Major, whose coon running days are a long time over, 'cause he is just too blame old to run any more, saw his chance. When that door came by him, he just hopped on board and rode right along behind, just a howling and enjoying the chase like he used to do."

"When I got home a couple of hours later, your Aunt Molly May dun told me, in no uncertain terms, that she was not going to use no outhouse without a door on it even if we do live a fur piece back in the piney woods. So, I had to fetch my gun to go run down Old Blue. It took me several hours to run that hound down. He must have chased that coon over half the county. I could hear him just a-howling up a storm. Old Major was adding his part. That old coon was a smart one, he kept changing directions and doubling back where he had already been. Finally, Old Blue treed him and I caught up with them."

"That chain was still on Old Blue, and what was left of the door was still dragging along behind. To my surprise, there sat Old Major acting like he had treed that coon all by himself. I had me a problem. I could not bring that door back and carry Old Major also, him being too old to walk that far by himself, besides that door was in pretty bad shape. I probably could not fix it up anyway."

"So I took the chain off the door and wrapped it around Old Blue's neck, so it would not fall off or get tangled in something. He drug it out there so he should have to carry it back to the house. I carried Old Major and the door, or what was left of it, stayed there in the woods."

"Your Aunt Molly Ann told me again in no uncertain terms that she still was not going to use no outhouse without a door, unless she just has to. Although, since we have nothing else, she has to, or go in the woods. So, I had to come and buy boards and hinges." said Uncle Elmer as he rose to go.

"Nice jawing with you, Nephew. You get shut of this here place, then y'all come on up to the old piney woods and we can sit a spell and palaver some more, you here? I hear you a 'coming I just might shoot that old coon and make you a coon skin cap just like old Daniel Boone." And with that, he breezed out the door not even waiting for a goodbye from Adrian.

As tough as he was, Uncle Elmer did not like sorrowful goodbyes.

A couple of the watchers walked over to the bed. One of them asked Adrian, "Is your Uncle always like that?"

"Pretty much," replied Adrian. "You can't believe hardly anything he tells you, but he is the most entertaining person I know. I am not sure if he can tell a straight story, he just prefers to describe life in his own unique way. I think a lot of what he says might have a grain of truth in it, but Uncle Elmer likes to embellish it into a much more interesting story. That story about Big Bubba I have heard before as true, but not nearly so interestingly. He could turn the story about a walk across a parking lot, into the most outlandish tale you ever heard. That is just who he is. But underneath all that malarkey is one of the most caring and loving persons you will ever meet. Also, I know for a fact, that Cousin Velma May is only slightly blond, and is working on a Masters at Texas A. & M. Uncle Elmer is really very proud of her. But he does not let facts get in the way of a funny whopper. Also, he chooses to use his kin in his stories so, other people will not get offended. Lot of folks are real thin skinned now days. I will tell you, that he was just what I needed to cheer me up, on what started out to be one of the most gloomiest days, since I have been this hospital of yours."

"I will grant you one thing," said one of the nurses. "You certainly have some of the most interesting relatives visiting you that I have ever met since I have been working in this hospital, and I have been here awhile. Which reminds me, we had better get busy before Nurse Hopkins catches us," the first nurse commented.

"Yeah! If she catches us a lollygagging around, she will skin our hides," claimed one of the ladies whom he recognized as one of those that delivered and picked up the food trays from the kitchen.

"From the sound of her talk I think that lady has some country in her from somewhere," thought Adrian.

Adrian lay thinking of all he had just heard. It took a while to absorb a visit from Uncle Elmer. Mother says I have his gift of gab, but I don't think anybody has anything like his gift of telling tall tales and making them sound as if they really happened or could have happened. He leaves you trying to figure out what part was real and what part was made up. Also, he leaves you cheered up, and a lot to laugh about. I needed that today.

In his "cover prayer" that night Adrian prayed.

Dear Lord you knew
I was not feeling good today,
Thank you for sending Uncle Elmer.
Please forgive him for all his lying, Lord.
I don't think he means it as a lie,
He is just telling things in a way,

To make a good story out of it.
Inside he is really a good man.
Help him to keep Aunt Molly happy.
Please bless Mother and Father,
Lee, Ann, and Edmond.
Help and heal all us kids in this hospital,
Especially that girl that cried all last night.
Lord could you have somebody,
To tell her about you, Jesus.
I want to ask You to make me,
Clean in my heart.
And forgive me all my sins.
Lord I want to get well and go home.
Just between you and me, Lord,
I am not as big and brave,
As I try to sound.
Actually, I am sick, tired, and scared.
I want to get well real soon.
Amen! Amen!

Chapter Twelve
Day 31: [Mon.] Filling In Mother

After the emotional high of Saturday, Sunday had been a real drag. Adrian had nothing to take his mind off the pain. The IV had greatly eliminated the number of times he was stuck with a needle for a while, but then the doctor had decided to pull the IV and go back to needle injections yesterday, Sunday. That was not a decision Adrian understood. However, he understood little of what the doctors were doing, except he still hurt no matter what they did.

He had another Angel dream Sunday night after he said his prayers and went to sleep. He was remembering the dream when Mother came in. Boy, was he glad to see her! He could hardly wait to tell her of the visit from Uncle Elmer.

Mother was surprised that Uncle Elmer had come this far out of the Piney woods just to see Adrian. She said he could have found the supplies he wanted much closer to home. Mother said there beat a heart of gold beneath all that bark and malarkey.

Adrian also told Mother about the candy stripper, Polly. Adrian told mother that he thought she was real kind, she listened to all he had to say, had some terrible but funny jokes, and was kind of pretty.

"Well then," mother said "you can show her that you got your name in the newspaper." Then mother handed him a copy of the article that said he was the third polio patient in Harris County, for the start of the 1946 polio season. It said, that was the same number of Polio Cases as reported at this time the previous year.

"Why does something bad have to happen to you to get your name in the newspaper," questioned Adrian.

"Well, it does seem like that," was the reply.

"Hey, Mother! I had another Angel dream last night!" excitingly proclaimed Adrian.

"What was it this time? Do you remember it? Most of the time you tell me you had a good or bad dream, but you can't remember any or most of what you dreamed." Mother queried him.

"I sure do this time," replied Adrian. "I dreamed I was walking in a nice wooded area, like a park or something. I heard a stream up ahead. When I came close enough to see the small stream, I noticed an Angel just sitting on a fallen tree trunk. It looked like the same Angel I saw before. The top of the tree trunk stuck out over the edge of the water."

""I said, "Hello Mr. Angel Sir!"""

"Hello Adrian. You can call me Silver Wing. How are you today?" the Angel asked.

"Well can you believe it? I feel just great," I said and I actually did. No fooling.

"What are you doing here?" I asked.

Silver Wing, answered me, smiling," and said, "just waiting here for you."

"Shouldn't you be up in the clouds somewhere, playing on a harp, whatever that is?"

"What made you ask that?" the angel asked.

"Somebody told me once that all angels do is sit

around on clouds and play harps." I said, smiling broadly. "So, do you do that? Can you play a harp?"

"You know, I don't know. I never tried. Oh course, I could if **He** wanted me to." answered Silver Wing reflectively.

"**He** who?' asked I.

"Why **He** is **God the Father**. I do only what **He** wants me to do and nothing else," replied the Angel.

"That sounds neat." I said. "I wish I only did what God wanted me to do."

Then I asked, changing the subject; "So, why are you waiting here for me?"

"I just wanted to visit with you, let you get to know me, also talk to you and let you see me. Remember, you said you wanted to see me again." he said.

I did not know how he knew that, but I did not dare to ask.

"Do you want to walk along the stream and talk?" the Angel asked.

"Sure, why not," I said.

We walked and talked. I asked a lot of questions. The Angel gently answered them all, one by one. While walking, I picked up small stones and tried to skip them across the water. The angel said skipping stones only worked where the water was not flowing, like on a pond.

After a while I asked him, "How come I see you now, but I never saw you before that last time."

"Well, you wanted to, I wanted you to, and most important, **God** wanted you to." Silver Wing replied.

"Why did **God** want me to?" I asked

"We don't ask why **God** wants something," he sort

of sternly rebuked. Then he continued. "Besides, when one is dreaming, you can do lots of things you can't do when you are awake."

"Am I dreaming?" asked I.

"Yes, you are," Silver Wings answered.

"Now that is really weird. I am dreaming and I know I am dreaming." I said, as I scratched my head in wonder.

"You can do all sorts of things in a dream," commented Silver Wing.

"Yeah! Like what?" I questioned.

"Well, let me see! How about jumping across this stream?" he asked. He knew boys liked to do athletic feats of daring.

"No way! You're kidding, right?" I asked excitedly, "That's impossible."

"Here, hold my hand and we will get a running start and give it a go. Okay?" the Angel said, as he offered me his hand.

"We backed up and took a running start and jumped. We landed lightly on the opposite shore." I said, "Now, that was super cool! Can we do it again?"

"Maybe some other time. I have to go now. There is a lesson here you need to think about. I will give you a hint. It has to do with doing the impossible depends on who is holding your hand. I just wanted to visit with you and let you know I am around. You see **God** wanted you to know that he is looking out for you all the time and to not be afraid. Know that he loves you, no matter what." the Angel said.

"I remembered the Bible said a whole lot about not being afraid every time an angel showed up. But somehow I was not afraid with this Angel."

"Then Silver Wing flew up in the air. He turned and waved to me before he flew away. Then I woke up. It was still night, so I went back to sleep." I finished feeling sort of wishful.

Mother quoted from the Bible, "... young men will see visions and old men will dream dreams. Perhaps this means you are getting old."

"Mother you're teasing me." Adrian protested.

"Yes, I was, although a vision is sort of like a dream. Anyway, dreaming of angels has got to be okay," Mother smilingly said. "I think I would like to dream of angels sometime."

"Mother," Adrian said changing the subject as he so often did. "I been thinking a lot, and I need to tell you something Lee and I did last year when we lived out at the farmhouse. I was afraid you would get mad and never let us climb trees again, if I told you. You know how much we like to climb trees. I remembered you said you climbed trees when you were a girl. I can never look at a tree that I don't think about how good a climbing tree it is or is not. Anyway, I made Lee promise never to tell you, but I kind of think I need to' now."

"What in the world did you two boys do?" Mother said, with sort of trembling in her voice. "If it is this serious, I am not sure I want to know. But you had better get it off your chest."

"I call it **My Great Tree Adventure.** You remember that beautiful old tree at the farmhouse that had the gate hooked on to it? It was perfect for climbing. How could any red-blooded boy my age resist climbing it? It was near the edge of the woods and not far from the converted goat shed just begged us to climb it. You know, I had been up in it before this day, but not too far. This day, Lee had begged to climb with me, and I let him. We did all right at first. I climbed with Lee right behind me. We got up really high. You could see the rice paddies on the next farm over. The mail box at the end of our driveway was as plain as could be, although it looked really small. I told Lee that we were higher than I had ever been before. Up that high, the tree swayed in the breeze. That was exciting."

"I am smaller than you are. I bet I could get higher," Lee told me.

"I really knew better, but I decided to let him try. **We** could brag <u>we</u> went clear to the top of that big old tree," I thought. "That would be something to brag about."

"Lee edged past me and went up about another three feet. His feet were right about even with my head. Just as I was telling him to stop, I heard and saw the limb he was standing on start to break. He started sliding down and I wrapped my arms around him when he got even with me. The limb I was on started to give way with the weight of both of us. We slid down another two or three feet with him on one side of that main limb and me on the other hanging on to each other for dear life. I don't really know how far, because I was really, really scarred. It took us about half an hour to get back down on the ground. We just sat there breathing hard, for the longest. I told Lee that brag or no brag we could never tell anyone what we had done. If you or Father ever found out you would skin us alive, especially me, because I should have known better."

"I know I should have told you before, but I was afraid to. If you want to punish me now, I will understand 'cause that could not be much worse than knowing I had kept it from you."

Mother said, "It is true you should have told us of this when it happened. You should have never done anything so dangerous in the first place and risked your brother's life as well as your own. But I think you have been punished enough, just thinking and worrying about it," Mother scolded. "I am glad that your conscious has prompted you to confess your wrongdoing. This was what you needed to do. I am sure you figured it out that you should have done it a long time ago. But now that has been done, and I forgive you, so don't let it bother you anymore. The Good Lord knows you have enough other problems to think about. It seems the **Good Lord**, (she always thought and spoke of **Him** by that name), is sending you some great people to take your mind off your problems. Of course, I also thank the **Good Lord** for the people here in the hospital that are trying to take care of you and get you well." She had a look of both pity and understanding on her face.

Mother told Adrian she had one more thing to do before she left to go home. She said that she had come from home prepared for a task: that was to clean and take Adrian's toys, home. She had brought a large bag and some kind of home remedy of cleaning fluid. Adrian thought it smelled like either Clorox or vinegar. He could not tell which. It made his room smell something like *"strip everything day"*, but not quite. He would miss his toys but, since he could not play with them, he believed they would be a lot better off clean and at home. It seemed like this old hospital made everything in his life different and unnatural.

Shortly after that, Adrian's mother had to leave. She was leaving with mixed feelings. She was very sad that her son was in this hospital with this crippling and killer sickness. But she also believed that the Good Lord was watching over her son. True she did not understand why all this was happening. But her's was a simple country faith.

That night Adrian prayed:

Dear Lord thank you for giving me,
Such a good Mother and Father.
Please watch over them and,
Help them not feel so bad about me being here.
Also please bless Lee, Ann, and Edmond,
And all my other kin ' cause I sure got a lot
Oh Yeah Lord! Will you also bless,
All the other people in this here hospital,
And all the Doctors and Nurses and
All the other people that done work here.
I thank You again for the neat Angel dreams,
I sure do like them 'cause they are so cool.
Also, they sure do seem real.
Thank you that I can remember them.
And by the way thank you for,
Helping me to tell Mother about,
My "great tree adventure".

I don't mean to be bad,
You already know I sin,
Please clean me up
And forgive me the sin I do
I have forgot for a while, but
Please bless and protect all the missionary kids.
Well, I guess I will go to sleep now,
So, goodnight
And Amen!

Sleep did not come to Adrian as quickly as he would have liked. It had started to rain realty hard. In fact, it was what his country kin called, a Frog Strangler and a Gully Washer. Now if you know your Texas Rains a Frog Strangler is a lot worse than a simple raining cats and dogs. It can really pour with lots of lightening and wind.

However, Adrian had had a rough day and finally dozed off to a restless sleep.

Chapter Thirteen
Day34: [Thur.] Fathers Explained

    Well, it was Thursday, and as eagerly expected, in came Polly. "I been looking for you all day," was the first thing Adrian said. "I thought I saw you pass by in the Hall a lot earlier today, but I guess it was not you."

    "Well, it could have been me," Polly replied, with a chuckle in her voice. "I have been in the hospital quite a while today."

    "I have been seeing the other two patients in this section of this floor, that the hospital has designated temporarily as the polio area. I guess this whole floor will be a polio wing if it goes like it did last year." this time with a sadness in her voice.

    "Two more like me?" Adrian questioned. "Can you tell me about them?"

    "Well, they have polio as you do, but I would not say they are a lot like you. In many ways, they are not at all like you. You know already that everybody is different. I can only tell you a little, (hospital rules) but let me see what I think I can tell you."

    "Just down the hall to your right is a girl about six. She has been here about two months. They had to put her into an Iron Lung last week. She is pretty scared. Her name is Faith Hope Miller. Her dad comes to see her mostly. Seems there is something wrong with her mom that keeps her from getting out and visiting much. She has made it a few times when she gets a caregiver, they hired for the mother to bring her. Her Father is a very brave fireman. In fact, he is a local hero because of the number of times he has saved people from very dangerous fires, even some important people once. Because he works four days on and three days off, he gets to visit a lot." Polly paused to get her breath.

"Now on the left is a boy named Freddie Alberto Von Brawn," Polly recited.

"Boy that is a mouthful of name," commented Adrian.

"Right. He is about eleven. He also is in an iron lung. He has been here for over four months. He is not doing very well. His father is some kind of general in the Army. The other day when I saw him in his uniform, he had all kinds of metals and ribbons on it. He must also be a brave and important soldier. Freddie's mother comes when she can. I think they have several other children," Polly finished her description.

"Well, you ready for your Jokes?" questioned Polly, quickly changing the subject.

"I don't know if I am ready or not, and remember these are your jokes not mine, but go ahead and shoot," was his reply.

"Did you hear about the rooster that was really super Lazy"

Adrian, "OK how lazy was he."

"He was so lazy that in the morning he would

wait for the other roosters to crow, then he just nodded his head.

"Oh Brother" laughed Adrian.

"Why did the Elephant cross the road?"

"Why"

"Because he did not want to be mistaken for the chicken."

"Not more chicken crossing the road jokes please. But that was not much funnier than the other ones." commented Adrian.

"OK, how about another elephant one," Polly asked.

"Sure!" was the answer.

How do you hide an Elephant in a strawberry patch?
"That is ridiculous. You can't hide and elephant in a strawberry patch!"
Sure, you can. Just paint his toenails red.
"That would not work."
"Did you ever see an elephant in a strawberry patch?"
"No!"
"See there, it worked. He was there, you just could not see him."
"OK, you got me on that one. That was pretty

good," Adrian had to admit.

"One more," Polly said.

"What do you call an Elephant that does not matter?"
"What"
"Irrelevant"

"Now that was funny," Adrian admitted.

Adrian was smiling about Polly's not-so-funny jokes. They were kind of funny, and you seldom find a grown-up that would tell a kid, jokes.

Adrian 's active mind went back to what Polly had said about the other two polio kid's dads.

"Polly, you were saying those other two kids have brave and heroic dads," reflected Adrian.

"Well, I guess I said something like that. I was just telling you what I heard and saw." Polly said, defensively.

"Well, my father is not a hero fireman or policeman, and he was never in the army. They never drafted Him. I don't know how brave he is, but then his life is one with the bark on. He is a little tough on us kids sometimes. Most of the times we deserve what we get, at least I know I do. And I don't know how brave he is but as far as I am concerned, he is just great." Somehow, Adrian felt he needed to defend his father.

"Well, a boy ought to be proud of his dad. What do you mean that your dad's life had the bark on?" Polly asked.

"I think my father's hard life started with my father's dad, you know, my grandpa." Explained Adrian.

He was getting a little defensive of his father.

"My grandfather got a divorce from his first wife and moved away from her and their two kids, I don't know why.".

"He remarried to a second wife, who was my father's mother. She died one night when my father was just three years old. She was literally scared to death by a terrible lightning storm. They say that lightening was striking the ground all around the house. My grandpa was not home because the bridge was washed out over the creek on the only road that led to their house. The stream was a raging torrent. It was good that a sister of hers was visiting." My father was raised for a while by his mother's sisters.

Then grandpa married a third time and had three more children. The third wife had as much bark as grandpa. She is tough.

Father says, "she is as tough as nails and can outlast a muleskinner."

She worked on the railroad some with Grandpa, before she started having kids.

"We call her Mam-Maw. My father sometimes did not get along too well with her. He ran away from home and went to stay with his mother's sisters a couple of times. Sometimes, he also worked on the railroad with Grandpa. I guess that is where he got his fascination for trains."

"He only finished the ninth grade in country schools. He wanted to learn but could not stay in school. Now he reads everything he can get his hands on. He is always quoting something he read somewhere. He settled down after he married my mother. He wanted a family. I guess because of his lack of education and country background, he has had lots of jobs. It seems when there is a layoff, he is the first to go. Also, he does not like to be pushed around or looked down on as some sort of a country hick. He does not look for trouble, but he sure will not take a lot of guff off people. Not that he fights or causes trouble, but he will just quit the job and go find another. We also had to move a lot."

""He never was in the service, and he never has been what some people consider an important person. I have heard him say, "I am just a hard-working stiff!" I am not sure why he says he is stiff. He gets sore, but he seldom gets stiff.""

"My dad is a strong disciplinarian. He is rough with the belt. I would much rather get a whupping from my mother than my father. As for me, I have gotten several, Okay, a bunch, but seldom for the same thing twice. My Father's corrections mostly make a point that you are not soon to forget."

"For example, one time we were on a trip back to the piney woods, to the town of Saratoga, Texas. That is the town near where I was born and where my Mam-Maw and my Grandma Rose still live. We go to visit, now and again. Ann, Lee, and I were in the back seat. Lee and I were bored, and so we started fussing, and picking, and poking each other. To be honest, it was mostly me picking on him just to make him holler. My Father knew what was going on in the backseat. In fact, he had told us to cut it out, but we had started it up again. Father stopped the car at the bottom of this hill and told me to get out of the car. Standing on the side of the road, my father told me that if I could not behave riding in the car, perhaps I should try walking for a while. Then he got back in the car and drove on up over the hill, out of sight. There I was, standing on the side of the road, way out in the country, miles and miles from everywhere, and all alone. Well, there was one old brown and white cow out in the field, but she was not paying me any attention and certainly was not going to be of any help. I suddenly realized how lonely you can get when you are all alone. Even a pesky brother around, would right then, look really good. I started up that hill and climbed and climbed it seemed that it was a mile high. Mother said later, when I was talking to her about it, that is was less than a quarter of a mile high."

"When I got to the top, after what seemed like hours, just a little way out of sight from the bottom, there was my father waiting on me. Mother said he was watching me from the top of the hill the whole time, but I sure did not know that."

"He asked if I thought I could behave in the back seat now?"

"Yes Sir!" I said humbly.

""He said, "Get in the car!" The lesson was not lost on Lee either. Neither one of us said hardly a word till we got to Saratoga.""

""From that time on, all he would have to do when we kids were acting up in the car was to say, "You kids want to walk?' He would have instant silence and behavior in the back seat.""

"Once we lived on a street in a neighborhood that

had several houses on each side of us and across the street. Father at that time was working at night, and us kids were supposed to play quietly outside. Well, I came up with this game that I would chase Lee and bark like a dog. I can't remember what the point of the game was, but I sure remember the outcome. I would chase him around the house and up and down the street barking at the top of my lungs. At the time, it was great fun. Father sent Mother out to tell me to cut out all the noise, a couple of times. I slowed down for a short time. But then I would forget and start up again. All of a sudden, I saw Father stranding in the doorway."

"So, you want to bark, do you! Well, I can help you with that. I want you to run up and down this road and bark as loud as you can until I tell you to stop." Father ordered.

All of a sudden, barking like a dog was not near as much fun as before. Also, I began to notice that the neighbors had started looking out and standing in their doorways to see what is going on. I was embarrassed and ashamed. I don't remember how long it went on, it seemed like hours, but I was so glad when Father said I could stop.

"Father asked If I thought that I could play quietly now and let him get some sleep?"

"I promised that I surely could do that."

"I thought at the time that I would never bark like a dog again in my life. That was not true, but I never did it to the excess of that time and never when it would disturb other people. I confess I have made a lot of other noises of various kinds. I think I am really good at making animal noises. But I try to never disturb other people with them. Father taught me to be considerate of others."

"Another time, actually the same neighborhood, I was running in and out of the house by the front door playing chase or something with Lee. We had a screen door that Father had put a strong spring on that helped it to shut tight and keep the flies out of the house. I was just busting through it and letting it slam because I did not want to slow down the chase. Father had already told me a couple of times to not let the door slam. I would slow down for a couple of passes through the house. But then I would forget, and soon I was back busting through and letting the screen door slam shut. Sure, I knew better but, in the excitement of my great fun game, I could ignore good sense and his warning."

"Father showed up at the front door and strongly suggested that I practice opening and closing that screen door as quietly as possible, over and over. I must have opened and closed that screen door a couple thousand times, okay, hundreds of times. The rest of the time we lived in that house; I never could go out that door without being very careful to not let it slam. You know, even today I can't let any other door slam if I can help it, even if I am not the one about to do the slamming."

Polly said, "Well I am glad my Dad did not use that method of teaching with me. I do see, that it seemed to be effective with a rambunctious child like you seem to be.

You seem like you are a handful. The child psychologist at the college where I go would have a field day with you and your father's teaching methods. But, as far me, I guess, it seems to work with you, so I would tell your Dad to go for it."

"Thanks a lot. "Adrian remarked pretending offense.

"You know, Polly, the thing that my Father is a most firm believer in, is family and the Good Lord and **His** church. He says they, family and church, are, in a way, sort of the same. Father says at least they should be. He says that God had a family long before he had a church. That does not make the church unimportant. Maybe, the Church should be patterned after the family.
In a way they are related in scope. The big difference is you are not physically related to the people in the church. True they are related to you in the Good Lord. Father says that we should always stick by our family and help them any way we can. They may have a little bark on, but they are still family. Also, if they are really family, they will stick by you when you need help and celebrate with you when you are in good fortune. My Father says he don't have much use for church folks that don't act like family or that look down on other folks or don't behave like family. I really believe like my Father and want to be like him."

"Say, Polly, I just remembered of something," piped up Adrian, as his mind shifted gears. "My mother brought in a newspaper clipping about me. It's in that yallar folder thing on the table. It's got a white page you can tape stuff on and a plastic cover sheet to keep things good and not get scratched up. Oh Yeah! By the way, did you notice that the toys are gone? Mother cleaned them up and took them home Monday night."

Polly picked up the article and read it. "I see this tells about you being the third polio case in Harris County this year. I guess that is kind of exciting to get your name in the paper. It is a shame that it usually takes something bad to happen before it gets in the newspaper."

"You know, my mother was talking about getting your name in the newspaper the other night. She said it was exciting. I said that thing you said, about mostly it happens when something bad is or has happened," Adrian repeated.

"Then mother had to reminded me of one of Dad's quotes,

"If there was no bad news there would be no news at all in the papers!"

"This was also bad news, but I did get my name in the newspaper another time a long time ago. It was before Ann was born. I think it was just after we moved to the city. Anyway, Father was driving in our car with only Lee and myself in the back seat and Him and Mother in the front seat."

"It seems that Father started to make a left turn just as a big eighteen-wheeler started to pass him. The eighteen-wheeler hit the left side of our car and, among other damage, took off the left rear door, and our car wound up in a deep ditch. The eighteen-wheeler was going so fast that somehow it jumped the ditch and hit a grocery store in one of those shopping malls places.

Mother, Lee, and the truck driver had to go to the hospital. The newspaper said Father and myself, <u>by name I might add</u>, were okay. I don't 'member 'nough about that accident, but I do remember riding in the car without the door. You could see everything go by real clear without a door; trees and cars and the road and everything. Father had to tie Lee and me down to the rear seat with a piece of rope, so we would not fall out until he could go to the junk yard and get another door. It was a different color than the rest of the car, but he fixed it really good, and it worked fine. Mother still has that newspaper clipping, also. She will probably put this one with it. It seems important to her to save it. In fact, my mother saves a lot of stuff. The newspaper clipping is special. When a country person gets their name in a paper, especially a big city newspaper, like a Houston paper, you notice it."

"I can understand that," Polly said. What she thought was, "To each his own."

"Speaking of noticing things, I just noticed the time. I have been at the hospital all day. I really got to go. I have to stop at a burger joint and get something to eat before I get home. No offense but hospital food just does not do anything for me."

"I understand. Too bad you could not smuggle me a good juice hamburger and some fries in to here, but then I probably could not eat it," Adrian sadly reflected. "At least I can enjoy the thoughts of eating them."

"Well, good night kid! and as my Mom used to say **Sleep tight and don't let the bedbugs bite**, Polly said as she breezed out the door."

"Haw! A bed bug would starve to death in a place

like this, as much cleaning as they do in here." Adrian chuckled to himself. He did remember that his own mother often told him that same saying.

That night he prayed;

Dear Lord Jesus I thank you for sending Polly.
Please forgive me for griping about the food,
I just wish I could eat it more.
Most of the time I can hardly eat it.
That meatloaf stuff they had today,
Was not too bad.
Please bless all my family,
Especially Mother, Father,
Lee, Ann, and Edmond.
I thank you again for all that You do for me.
Amen!

Chapter Fourteen
Day 36: [Sat.] Visits: The Best & Worst

The sun was shining right into Adrian's eyes as he awoke. He was still sleepy, but he knew that it would not be long till some nurse would be ***taking his vitals*** as he had learned they called it. Did they not know that his ***vitals*** were getting some real rest without somebody poking and turning you? Then he remembered that thing last night when the bedpan did not get to him fast enough and all the trouble that caused. It must have been an hour before everything got straightened out, and he could go back to sleep. He did not like it, but he had learned to live with it. He remembered that taking a bath in a number 3 washtub, in the middle of the floor, by the wood burning stove, at the old farmhouse, used to be the most embarrassing time he could think of. Boy that was nothing compared to this hospital.

The bright sunshine reminded him of the really beautiful full moon he kept seeing every time he woke up last night. It was really, really big. And it looked like it was shining. He figured it must be clouds or something but it really looked like it was shining. Of course, he had learned in school that the moon was sort of like a mirror. It did not shine. It just was a reflection of the sun shining on it. The more the light of the sun the moon reflected, the brighter it made the moon look. A full moon was when the earth got out of the way, and you could the whole moon. Also, sometimes the moon was closer to the Earth than at other times and looked bigger. All this he had studied in school just last year.

This also reminded him of a Sunday School lesson. The teacher had said the more the **Son of God** shines on our life, the better we are, and look, and feel.

Adrian's thoughts took, a bunny trail. You know, I sure wish that the **Son of God** would hurry up and shine on me, so I can start looking and feeling better. I would like **Him** to shine on me like that big old Moon shined last night 'cause right now I don't feel like I am shinning at all. I wish He would shine right into this room like that big full moon. "You know something, if anybody heard me talking about what I am thinking about, they would think I had flipped my rocker." Adrian thought.

"It would be good to go to Sunday School again. Father is a Baptist, and if there was not a Baptist church near the place we lived, we did not go so much. And we moved a lot." This was where Adrian's active wandering mind had taken him.

While he was thinking about moonlight and stuff, in walked Aunt Stella May and Uncle John Boy Brewster. The Brewsters had left his five cousins with Mother so they could come up to see Adrian. They had an older girl, then a set of twin boys, and after that, a set of twin girls. When they all got together the kids had a ball.

"Well, boy! when you going to get out of here and come home? Both your brothers and your sister are really missing you. Also, all your cousin's kind of miss you as well," asked Uncle Billy Bob, knowing Adrian had no real answer.

"I wish I knew. Today would not be soon enough to get out of here," was Adrian's answer with a tear in his voice.

"Just this morning, Lee said that he wished you would come home so he could have somebody to pester and pick on him," Aunt Stella May put into the conservation.

Adrian's logical mind kicked in and he asked, "Uncle John Boy, all the nurses and doctors call this the Children's Ward. If me and all the patients up here are children, and if nobody is contagious, why can't my brothers and sister and my cousins come up to see me? I miss seeing them something terrible."

"Adrian, it is the Children's Ward. And true it is called the Children's Ward because there are only children here. And while nobody is contagious right now, they are all sick or they would not be here. Sick people have germs. Germs make other people sick. Children get sick easier than grownups. You don't want any of your family getting sick also, do you?" Explained Uncle John Boy.

"Oh no!" exclaimed Adrian. "I guess I was just not thinking. It is just that I want to see them so much."

"How have you been feeling?" Asked Aunt Stella Mae, thankfully changing the subject.

"I have bad days and then really bad days," Adrian answered.

"No good days?" was the question.

"Not really in the way I feel physically. I have had some great visits from my relatives. Mother may have told you that Aunt Lolla came up here and brought me some real neat toys and almost got thrown out by the Head Nurse. Also, Uncle Elmer came up and told some real whoppers, like he always does. He attracted quite a crowd. Had Nurse Kincade been here he might have been kicked out also. Then there is this candy striper named Polly that comes on Thursday, she tells dumb jokes and talks with me a lot. Of course, Mother comes a lot, but you know about that. All these visitors really help me not to think about the pain and hurt so much," Adrian said, stopping to catch his breath. "Now y'all have come."

"I guess I like visits more since I been in here that I ever did before," Adrian said as his wandering mind picked up that thread of thought and ran with it.

"Do you know the worse visit I think I ever got?" he asked.

"No, what was that?" they asked.

"It was one time when Mam-Maw came to visit. Now as you probably know she chews tobacco. And, of course, she has to spit a lot. At home, she spits into an old coffee can that looks like it is as old as she is. Or if she is sitting on the front porch, I have seen her spit all the way out into the yard. She is quite a spitter. She is probably the worlds champion. But that can she uses stinks to high heaven."

"Well, she had to come to the city to see a doctor, so she stayed with us a few days. She took over Lee's and my bed, so we had to move into the living room and sleep on a pallet. Also, she also took over Mothers almost new rocking chair right in the middle of the living room. Mostly she sat and rocked while she was here. She told

Father that she had to have a coffee can to spit in. Thank goodness she left her old one at home. He got her one out of the trash can that he had finished up the day before. She sat it right by the rocking chair and rocked and spit. She also hollered a lot, not spoke, at us kids, but we expected that, as it was just her way. I think Aunt Lolla learned hollering from her."

"Anyway, Lee and I got to playing chase in the house as the weather was bad outside. Lee ran through the living room and tipped Mam-Maws coffee can with the edge of his foot. The can went scooting across the floor and, as luck would have it, stayed upright. Naturally, Lee got yelled at. I ducked out of sight so she would not see me and yell at me."

"Later, I took Lee into the other room and told him what a complete and total disaster <u>we</u> had just avoided."

"Avoided, heck," Lee said. "I just got yelled at, while you played it safe in the other room."

"That is true," I admitted. "However, that is not near the worse part! Just think what would have happened if you had kicked over that awful coffee can. You know who would have had to clean up that mess? Right! You and me. It gives me the willies just thinking about it. Plus, we have to sleep in that room. The smell is bad enough now. But then if that had of happened! I don't even want to think about it. At least at night she takes that can to the bedroom with her. So, from now till Mam-Maw leaves, we don't play in the living room no matter what. Agreed?" He agreed.

Adrian was on a roll so he continued. "The best visit I can remember was when we went to see my Aunt

Annie Lee Forester and her spinster daughter, Molly Alice. They were another of my Father's birth mother's kin. Aunt Annie Lee is the oldest of the Martinson girls. She still lives on the farm where my father built his log cabin. He later sold the cabin, and someone went back in the woods and hauled it out. I saw it once, but now it has rooms added on and does not look much like a log cabin."

"I love seeing the farm on which I was born. The house they Aunt Annie Lee has lived in for ages, it is sort of an unusual house now-a-days. When it was built, the house and the kitchen were two separate buildings. They said it was built that way, in case the kitchen caught on fire, it would not burn the house down. Now days, they have a porch and a roof between the two. It still has no sides, but you can go one to the other without getting wet when it rains and such."

"Us kids had been playing outside till super was ready. Aunt Annie Lee was cooking on a big four-hole wood, cook stove. Father was teasing Molly Alice about her beau coming calling. She was busy denying any beau came by and if one did, she would get the rifle and send him packing. Evidently, it was an old family joke and they were enjoying themselves tremendously."

"I noticed that Aunt Annie Lee was hearing something outside. She went over to the back door and kicked it open with her bare foot. She only wore shoes when she was going into town or traipsing through the woods or hunting."

"There is that mangy hog in my corn field again," she said. In one easy motion, she reached down and picked up a 1938 Model Red Rider BB Gun and started shooting that hog from the hip. She never missed and keep hitting him in the rear with those BB's. He ran as fast as his short fat legs could carry him out of that corn field."

"I had never seen anything in real life like it. I just stood there with my mouth open staring. None of my movie cowboy heroes could ever beat that. She acted like there was nothing to it and went back to her cooking. What a shot!"

"My father told me later that her and her husband had carved that farm out of those Piney Woods many years before. They had, together, hunted bear, dear, wolves, raccoon, possum, wild hogs, squirrels, and, occasionally a bob cat and other critters in those woods. She had several real rifles over the mantel in the living room. Father, said she was just as good a shot with them as that BB gun. He said he had at one time been a pretty good shot himself with some of those same guns."

"For me that was a real exciting visit." Adrian recounted.

"Well now, that does sound like you had a great visit. However, I have something here I think you will enjoy today during our visit. I know you especially like jokes and funny things, so we brought you some copies of signs we found for you." said Uncle John Bob. "Like this,"

I Checked In To The Hokey Pokey Clinic & I Turned Myself Around.	**My Wife Said I Never Listen To Her, Or Something Like That.**
If Your Car Is Running I'm Voting For It	**Frog Parking Only All Others Will Be Toad**
This Is My Step Ladder I Never Knew My Real Ladder	**What Happens If You Get Scared Half To Death Twice**

"Not to be outdone, Aunt Stella Mae interjected, "I have a cousin who lives up in Waco. I have had occasion to visit her a lot lately. On the highway coming south, back from her house, there are two sets of those clever road signs put out by Brama Shave, about 50 miles apart. You know the ones that are a string of small signs ever so often along the highway? I just love to read them when we are traveling. We tell the kids to watch for them. Sometimes they do and sometimes they are so busy pestering each other, they totally miss them. Not only are those signs funny, but a lot of the time, they talk about highway safety in a humorous way. I should have copied down some of them to let you read them. They have them scattered all over the state.

"Sure I 'member them. Sometimes I don't get all the joke, because I forget the first part when I get to the last part. And sometimes we are past the first ones before I notice them. 'Course, if we go the same way often enough, I memorize where they are and learn the whole thing." Adrian interrupted.

Sally May overlooked the interruption and continued, "Well it seems another company has decided to give them some competition. On the side of the road going north about half way between the Brama Shave signs are some by Carter's Hair Oil. I don't really think they will catch on because the message is too long. It took me several times and trips to get it all down, but

what it said was really funny I think," said Aunt Stella May. "Here is what it said," then she read it to Adrian.

> I've been to a lot of places,
> But I've never been in Cahoots.
> Apparently, you can't go alone,
> You have to be in Cahoots with someone.
> I've also never been in Cognito, either.
> I hear no one recognizes you there.
> I have been in Sane.
> They don't have an airport,
> You have to be driven there.
> I have made several trips.
> Carter's Hair Oil

"Ha! Ha! That <u>is</u> really funny." said Adrian laughing.

"It hurts to laugh so hard but I can't help it. Also, my eyes are getting tired. The doctor says I might have to start wearing my glasses all the time," sighed Adrian.

"We are sorry Adrian, we just wanted to cheer you

up some." apologized Uncle John Boy.

"Oh no! don't apologize, I loved it. If I want serious, all I got to do is listen or talk to the doctors and nurses in this place. I have never been in a more serious place in my whole life. I don't believe some of the people here know how to smile. They look like they lost their last dollar."

"That reminds me of a story I heard on the radio recently," reminisced Adrian. "It seems that this couple Alfred and Gertrude lived a very frugal lifestyle. It was Alfred's tight budget. He was a real skinflint. He had a good job, but he took about twenty percent of his pay and put it under their mattress. They were married thirty-five years, and in all that time, Gertrude was not allowed to spend any money, except on what was absolutely needed. Being an obedient wife, she went along with it. Alfred made Gertrude **promise** that when he died, she would put all **his** money in his casket so he could buy his way into heaven. He finally died. Gertrude was a faithful wife who kept her word. That same day Gertrude took all the money out from under the mattress and went to the bank. She opened a bank account with the $35,000. Then she wrote out a check for the entire amount, made out to Alfred and the next day faithfully put it in Alfred's coffin. There's being tight with your money and there's handling in wisely."

Both Aunt Sally May and Uncle John Boy laughed at Adrian's story.

Adrian felt a wave of nausea pass over him and he was lying flat in bed. It must have shown on his face because both his Aunt and Uncle quickly asked him what was the matter.

"I am alright, I guess" he said weakly. "Sometimes I get sort of dizzy. I have been dizzied before. Like when we to go to the drive-in theater. Mother and Father let us go up front and play till the show starts. Of course, they have to wait till it gets dark enough to see the movie. They have this thing; we called a merry-go-round. Kids can get on it while other kids push it. If you are pushing, and it is going fast enough you can jump on and go round and round, till it slows down. Then we do it all over again. It is lots of fun. But, sometimes going round and round like that can make you so dizzy that you can hardly stand up for a while. When you stop and try to stand upright, your head is still going round and round inside. Lots of time you actually fall down. To be honest sometimes we got dizzy on purpose so we could fall down. You know it is one of those crazy things a kid does that is a lot more fun than when it happens and you are playing pretend than when you are not playing and it happens for real."

"Sometimes I feel dizzy like that in here. But what I really like at the drive-in playground is the fence. It is made of four-inch pipe That runs all the way across and separates the playground from the parking area. What I like to do is to walk on the top of the pipe, balancing as I walk along it. I am pretty also good at it, if I do say so myself."

Looking at her watch, Aunt Stella May said, "Oh my goodness, just look at the time. Sorry Adrian, we got to run. Those kids of ours have probably driven your mother up a wall by now. I know from experience, watching her's and that brood of ours, they are a double handful."

Gathering their stuff up they came to the bedside, Uncle John Bob shook Adrian's hand and Aunt Stella May kissed him on the forehead.

Later in his prayers Adrian prayed;

Jesus, you know all about my visits.
Both the one I had today
And the ones I talked about.
I thank you for the good ones,
Please forgive me for gripping,
About the bad ones.
Please forgive me for this sin,
Please make me white as snow inside,
Would you please hurry up?
And make me well again.
Cause I am really tired
Of being so sick.
I want to go on visits and such,
I ask you again to bless my family,
Each and every one.
I really do want to get well,
Jesus and go home.
I pray in Jesus Name.
Amen.

The 1938 Model Red Rider BB Gun

Chapter Fifteen
Day 38: [Mon.] Forty Questions, Sleep: Best & Worst

Adrian slowly woke up early. It seemed the sun was hardly up. What day was it? Adrian could not remember if it was the first of the week, the middle of the week, or the weekend. To be honest, he sort of judged the week by the visits of family and Polly. He knew they came on certain days. What went on in the hospital the rest of the time was boringly routine. The same, day in and day out. He tried and could not remember how long he had been in the hospital. It seemed like a very, very long time. Was his memory starting to play tricks on him?

His vomiting had stopped, but the headaches increased, or so it seemed. Was there every time he did not hurt? All his body hurt. Well, that was not quite true. The fact was, part of his body did not feel at all. It seemed that part of him was not there. He could reach over with his right arm, which hurt something awful, and rub his left arm with the right hand. It was like rubbing an arm belonging to somebody else, 'cause he did not feel anything in that left arm. It was all kinda scary. It was one of those things you can't really understand until it happens to you. He was lying there wondering about it, trying to understand it. Was he just imagining this absent arm business or was it real?

Emotionally, Adrian was feeling really out of sorts.

Actually, he was feeling downright grumpy. The pain and it's longevity had replaced his usual cheery outlook on life with a feeling of ***stop the world and let me get off***. This was a saying he had picked up from one of his uncles. He did not want to talk to anybody or see anybody or be around anybody; not his family, not Polly, just not anybody. But he that knew that would never work in this hospital. Here there were people, people, and more people. He just felt like griping about anything and everything.

Just at this moment, who should show up at his room but the two doctors he had in his mind started calling, ***Dr. B and His Shadow.*** It must be their day to visit. It seemed they came earlier and earlier each time and more and more often. Why did they have to come so early? He had never really been a morning person. He had always liked to stay up late and sleep in late. To be perfectly honest, he really did not get to sleep in all that late at home either. With other children in the house, and one of them almost a baby, someone was usually waking him up early. Why do babies always seem to wake up at the crack of dawn? The fact that they all slept in practically the same room in that small cabin did not help. One thing about the big old farmhouse, it was hard to keep all of it really warm, but Lee and him had a whole, big old room all to themselves.

Actually, he had to admit that on school days he had to get up early. In summertime, now that was what he liked in the sleeping department. Sleep in nearly every morning, at least most of the time. One thing at home...he usually got a decent night's sleep. When everybody went to bed, they stayed in bed and slept, but not so here.

"How are we doing today Adrian?" asked Dr. Billing, reading the name off the chart and handing it back to Dr. Jones as he starts examining Adrian.

Adrian knew that the Dr. Billings really did not expect an answer, or even consider Adrian as a person...just a patient. Adrian answered the doctor with, "I don't know how **We** are doing. I feel just lousy. I have no feeling in my left arm." Adrian said, sarcastically.

"How are **You** doing, Dr. B?" he asked the doctor.

Dr. Billing mumbled, "Oh, that's nice," as he kept on with his examination, which confirmed Adrian's suspicion that the doctor considered him as a patient, not a person.

He could have said, "The Green Cow jumped over the Yellow Moon Dressed in Pink Tights and holding a Red Umbrella!" which was ridiculous, and the doctor would have not even noticed."

Dr. Jones was studying Adrian's chart. "His readings show a decline in maneuverability, as well as a negative on food consumption. We had a positive for orange juice for a while, but I believe that it has caused a rash in the areas of the lower abdomen. Also, he has been complaining of more headaches and often shows a higher temperature than we like."

The doctors did their poking and questions as usual. But the examination took on what Adrian thought of as the ***40-question*** phase. "Do you hurt here? How about here? Are you hot? Are you cold? Do your headaches last long? Are they mostly at night? Do you feel numb? Where? How often? Are you hungry? How is your sleep?

How often do you feel numb? Where? Do you sleep best on your back, your stomach, your side?" The questions went on and on like that for what seemed to Adrian hours. It was not, of course.

Because of his bad mood, some of Adrian's answers were not so polite. They included answers like "Yeah! You done asked that a dozen times! What do you expect? Naw! Ugh Take it easy, will ya? I guess so." And other such rudeness, and ended with, "You done asking dumb questions yet?" To his credit there were a few Yes and No answers. But the polite answers, Yes Sir, or No Sir, that he had been taught all his life, were missing.

It seemed they were asking the same questions over and over but only in a different way. At least today **The Shadow** was taking notes.

Dr. Billings said, "We can try to depend more on the IV now for a while. Also start giving him a stronger pain medicine when he complains of excessive pain. As you know, much of our treatment of polio is still trial and error."

They had one more question for Adrian. "What do you have to say about the number and kinds of shots we have been giving you?"

The Shadow noted the instructions on the chart.

Trying not to sound like too much of a smart-alack, he gave this answer, "My mother always told me if you can't say something nice, don't say anything at all. So, I have nothing to say about your shots."

As experienced professionals, the doctors seemed not to notice the rudeness. They seemed to have gathered enough information to satisfy them that they could reach a conclusion. "I definitely think he has gone into phase 1," stated Doctor Billings, decisively. "While we can diligently work toward reversal, I think we must consider there being some nerve and muscle damage. Do you concur doctor?"

"I concur completely. I don't think there can be any other conclusion.," replied Dr. Jones.

They hung the chart back on the chart rack, complete with **The Shadow's** notes, for the nurse to type up later, and left the room still talking to each other. Adrian could hear that they had already switched their conservation to another patient.

Adrian just lay there. "Now, wasn't that an enlightening thought, Phase 1," he sarcastically thought to himself. He did not understand all that they said, but it certainly did not sound good, especially that part about nerve and muscle damage. He could not help but have tears in his eyes. He had been taught not to feel sorry for himself, but sometimes it was not an easy thing for a guy to do.

Last night had been another long restless night. He was not sleeping well at all. Besides, it was not natural for a guy to stay in bed all the day and night, normal was only when he was supposed to be asleep. Lately, he was not sleeping as well as he should have been. The sudden sharp pains he got from time to time did not help a lot. Neither did the night nurse coming in to check the chart, poke at him, or helping him relieve himself once or twice. It seemed that all his life he had always had to go to the bathroom sometime in the middle of the night at least once, long before he got here in this hospital. What was the matter with him? You would think a guy as old as he was would have outgrown that sort of thing. That was baby stuff.

As usual his bed did not feel really very comfortable, and last night was another night of rain and storm. There was lots of thunder and lightning that did not help his sleep. Was his morning going to be filled with thoughts of bad things? His father had told him when it seems your day is not going well, and all you seem to be able to think about are bad things, then <u>decide</u> to think of good things on purpose. Think of something, sometime, or someone you enjoyed or like.

"Good memories are great soap to wash away the blues."

Adrian began to remember that the best bed and the best night's sleep he ever had. It had to be that night the family spent at Mam-Maws back in the old Piney Woods three winters ago. The family had gone for a short visit. He remembered how cold it was in that old house, and that it had been a windy and rainy cold night.

The old house had only one stove, and it was in the front room. They had gotten rid of the wood burning stove a few years before. "Gone modern with a gas burning stove after the county had run gas back into our area." was Mam-Maw's brag. Lee and Adrian were given the bedroom furthest in back of the house that used to belong to Father's youngest sister before she grew up, got married, and left home.

Lee and Adrian quickly got dressed in their warm flannel pajamas and crawled into bed. Man, what a bed! It had a feather filled mattress and big feather pillows. When you lay down on that mattress, you sank down almost level deep.

For cover, there was a sheet and two big beautiful homemade quilts with all kinds of pretty, homemade patches sewn together to make all kinds of patterns. The country women, in that part of the woods, would take scraps of material left over from dresses they had sewed or swapped for and sew them into special patterns or designs.

Often the ladies would go to a quilting Bee and sew together. They sewed the quilt pattern they had pieced together, on top of a middle layer called batting and a bottom layer called the backing. It was a time of fellowship for them. They prided themselves in their homemade quilts and were known for them for miles around. Mother had said that some of her fondest memories as a girl was going to a Quilting Bee.

The lovely quilts covered the two small boys, so that they could hardly move. They had never felt snugger and warmer in their life. Rain had started to pitter patter on the tin roof overhead. At least that is what Father called that sound. To Adrian, it was one of the best, most restful, and lovely sounds he had ever heard in his life.

Adrian had just wanted to lay there and listen. He told Lee to shut-up and listen. True, he should have been more polite to his brother, but Lee understood. Adrian thought to himself there was no better place in the world right then, not even if it were a castle. He had drifted off to sleep listening to the falling rain.

Then he recalled a problem had developed. It had

nothing to do with the bed, it was the call of nature. Adrian waited, hopping it would go away, but knowing all along it would only get worse, not better. He remembered Mam-Maw's house did not have an indoor bathroom. There was only the recently repaired, big old outhouse about a hundred feet back of the house. Now each bedroom did have what they called a chamber pot. They were for use mostly at night or any other time one could not get to the outhouse, for whatever reason. At night when one did not want to make a trip to the outhouse in the dark, one could use the chamber pot. There was no moon out that night. He had recalled that, in the piney wood, if there was no moon or bad weather, dark meant really dark; black, inky, you can only see shadows, dark. There were no neighborhood lights, corner city or streetlights, and he did not have a flashlight here in these woods.

At about what Adrian imagined to be around four in the morning, the soothing rain on the roof had started to have another effect on Adrian, as he remembered. It only increased the urge. He really, really did not want to get out of that warm bed. The more he waited, the stronger the urge got. He would never live it down if he "wet the bed." The shame at his age would be unbearable.

Finally, shivering from the cold, he crawled out of the bed. The floor was like ice to his bare feet. The outhouse was a long way out there in the cold, dark, and rain. There was no way he was going to try that. So, then he was faced with another problem. To do his business in one of those tin chamber pots would send a message all over the house about what he was doing., He came to the conclusion the only other choice was to slip out on the back porch and do his business from the edge of the back porch, and try to not get wet from the rain. This he did, in record time, with the assurance not a living soul saw him then quickly ran and jumped back into that warm feather bed. Lee slept through the whole thing as he were on another planet. Adrian got warm again just about the time the rain on the tin roof put him back to sleep. He then finished a wonderful night's sleep, no worse for wear. Looking back, he thought it was a toss up to which he disliked more, that old tin chamber pot or the terrible hospital bedpan he had to put up with here in this hospital. His face turned red as he thought about the two.

There was something else that had happened on that trip that had made that visit special. He had almost forgotten but thinking about the bed and the night's sleep had reminded him of it. It was the last time he had seen his grandfather. The old fellow had passed away shortly thereafter. Adrian had always been a little shy around him if not slightly afraid. He was a very old man. He always seemed to Adrian to be a stern and serious-looking old man. The old fellow had given him a present. It was not a toy but a small ball peen hammer. It was to become a prized possession. Adrian decided to keep it till he was an old man then give it to his grandson, preferably one that would carry on the family name. It would go from grandfather to grandson to grandson, kinda neat like.

Nurse Kincade came in a little later to do chart work and the seemingly never-ending shots. She noticed that Adrian was now smiling, even as he would wince from time to time as he had a pain. She knew from experience that children in this stage of polio often experienced a lot of sudden pain. He was different from a lot of the other children she had worked with in her many years of nursing.

"Little Trooper, you are so pleasant. You seem to be always trying to smile and be friendly." remarked Nurse Kincade.

"I am afraid I was not so nice this morning when the two doctors were in here," he confessed. "I had another bad night, and I did not feel nice at all toward anybody especially those two, cold fish. They really rub me the wrong way. It is not because they are the source of all my shots and poking and turning and ordering of my misery. Okay, that may be a little unfair, but they are so ignore-ish. I know that is not a word, but they are. I feel when they are here, that I could be just as well as a piece of meat that they are looking over. They are like my uncle getting ready to cut up a hog he has killed and ready to butcher. I saw him do that once. Uncle was trying to figure which cut of meat he wanted to start on first. Sure, I know that is an exaggeration, but **Dr. B. and the Shadow** really get to me."

Nurse Kincade had to smile at the description of the doctors. While she disapproved of the disrespect, she did see the reason for it. They did work in such a manner that it really fit. Out loud, Nurse Kincade said, "You know Little Trooper, they have only the interest in helping you get well. It is nothing personal. They are that way with everybody."

"I am sorry, and I do know they are just doing their job, but I can't help feeling the way I do about them," was Adrian's confession. "I guess I should remember my father's quote when looking at those two doctors."

"And your father's quote is?' She questioned.

"If you only look for the bad, then all you will find is the bad."

My dad says if you are <u>only looking</u> for the bad in a situation, then all that you can find is the bad. You can not see any good, even when it is there, because you are only looking for the bad. If you are also looking for the good, then you can often find that also." repeated Adrian, as if he were repeating a lesson well learned after much repetition.

"I would say that your father is a wise man. And you are a wise son for listening to him." remarked Nurse Kincade.

"Well, I don't know if I am a wise son, I kinda doubt it, but I do know the doctors are trying to help me. But I do wish they were more...more...ugh, friendlier about it." stammered Adrian. Nurse Kincade finished her duties and went on about her rounds.

Adrian's mind jumped to the subject of probably his worse night's sleep ever. As fate would have it, that also was at Mam-Maw's house. A couple years before, the family had gone for a visit to Mam-maw's for a sort of family get together. This was occasioned because Uncle Roy, Father's younger brother was going to be home on leave from the Army. He was a favorite with Adrian, Lee and Ann as well as Mother and Father. He always made a big to do over the children and did magic tricks, like pulling nickels out of their ears and such.

Father's youngest sister came home with her husband and took her old room, so it would be a little crowded, therefore Lee and Adrian were to sleep on a pallet in the nice warm front room, so it would not be too bad. They often had to do this at Mam-Maw's when lots of family were there. Ann would sleep on a pallet in the room with Mother, Father, and Edmond. As it turned out, nobody got much sleep that night.

It had been one of the most scary and exciting times in his life. There came up a hurricane. They had known about it coming in from the Gulf of Mexico, but it was supposed to hit Louisiana. But hurricanes seldom do exactly what the weatherman thinks they are going to do. This one turned, and the center was headed right for the piney woods' country. Father had expected only a bad rainstorm, when we lift on the visit and we all so wanted to see Uncle Roy.

It started with the rain and wind. It was the hardest rain and the strongest wind Adrian had ever heard or seen. The old house began to shake like it was going to fall apart.

Mam-Maw said "This old house may shake and tremble but she has been in hurricanes before and she can take it. She has weathered some bad times, and she is still standing, just like me."

The roof sprang several leaks. The family put out pots and pans and buckets, anything that would hold water, even the chamber pots, all over the house to catch the drips. They saw all sorts of things fly by the windows. Every so often, something would hit the side of the house and, to Adrian, it sounded like it was going to come through the walls. This went on for the longest time, then everything sort of slowed down. The rain stopped and the wind died down. Adrian wondered what had become of the hurricane.

Uncle Roy said, "come outside," everybody did and looking up you could see the moon and stars.

"What happened?" Adrian asked Uncle Roy.

"This is the eye of the storm," was Uncle Roy's answer.

"Storms have eyes?" said Adrian, in wonder.

Uncle Roy answered, "That is what the weather people call the very center of the hurricane. All the air is whirling around and around a center. The bigger the hurricane, the bigger the center, usually."

"Oh no, does that mean that the rain and wind will be coming back?" questioned Adrian.

"Yes, only this time it will be blowing just as hard the other way. We need to empty all the buckets and things of water, so they can be filled up again very shortly. It will all be coming again." this was the orders from Uncle Roy. He had sort of taken over the operation, even if Father was the older brother.

Sure enough, the wind and rain started to build, and it was just as bad as before. It seemed that everything that had blown by going one way was coming back from the opposite direction.

Uncle Roy, who was a great kidder; told Ann, Lee, and Adrian that if the storm blew the porch away, he was going to leave also. Sure enough, the wind ripped off the front porch. Uncle Roy pretended to be preparing to go out the front door with the storm ragging, and leave as well. Adrian and Lee each grabbed one of Uncle Roy's legs and began to beg him not to go outside. Then he laughed and told them he was only kidding. No one got much sleep the rest of the night. The next morning the wind and rain had pretty much gone. The hurricane had moved further inland. They found the storm had knocked down several trees and really damaged the bridge at the end of the dirt road leading to Mam-Maw's house. This, in real life, gave understanding to that old saying that Adrian had heard most of his relatives say. When the promised to do something or be somewhere, they would say they would do it if

"The Good Lord Willing and The Creek don't rise."

No one was going to leave until someone got a way over the creek by repairing the bridge.

However, the most dramatic damage that stood out in Adrian's mind as damage, was what happened to the outhouse. When they walked around to the back yard, all they saw where the old outhouse had been, was a large hole. They found the old outhouse about three quarters of a mile from Mam-Maw's house. The recently repaired outhouse. That old outhouse had been well built. The damage was to part of the roof. The door was barely hanging on by the old leather hinges. It needed new metal hinges. It took the better part of a day to drag it back up to the house.

Mam-Maw said that as she had wanted to move it for some time anyway, so now was that time. She told the men to dig a new hole about six feet closer to the house and set the outhouse over that. Mam-Maw did not have a Sears Catalog, but she did have a Montgomery Ward's catalog. They were not as thick as a Sears, but they would do till she could get a Sears.

Mam-Maw told them that could use the dirt from the new hole to fill the old one. The old hole was filled with water, as well as other unmentionables. Adrian was glad for once that he was a little kid and did not have to help. That was the nastiest and worse smelling job that he could ever imagine. Somehow the men figured it out. Adrian said he did not even want to know how. In a couple of days, they all headed back to the living in the city. Thinking about that hurricane and other exciting times sure took his mind off the doctor's, the hospital, and his pain. The good thing about memories was the bad things no longer seemed as real, and the good things could be enjoyed all over again in your mind, Adrian was not sure how that all worked, but he was glad it did.

His prayers that night were:

Well, here I am again Lord Jesus.
I want to thank you for all the memories.
You have let me live in some good times,
You have let me live in some exciting times.
You have let me be kin,
To some good and strong country people.
They don't have much,
But they are rich in memories.
And they know how to make the best,
With what they do have.
Bad times and good times.

Help me make the best of the time,
I have to be in this here hospital.
Please make me strong,
Like you made them.
Please bless all my kinfolk,
Especially Uncle Roy.
Please forgive me for being,
Grumpy with the doctors this morning.
Could you make them be a little nicer?
I keep doing it Lord,
I want to stop sinning,
Since I can't stop on my own,
I sure could use your help.
Please forgive me.
And make me a better boy.
In Jesus' name I ask all this.
Amen!

Quilting Bee **Chamber Pot**

Chapter Sixteen
Day 41: [Thur.] Intro. To Iron Lung

Adrian's condition had taken a turn for the worse this last week. He had become very weak. His neck was so stiff that he had trouble turning his head. He had lots of back pain. Also, he had almost continual headaches. The polio had progressed to the paralysis stage. His left side was completely paralyzed. Not only could he not feel his left arm, but it had spread to his leg. He could not move them at all. His intake was back to the IV. When he tried to speak, his voice was strained and hoarse. He was at a stage where he required someone watching him around the clock. Nurse Sally had drawn the shift this morning.

Adrian was also sad because Polly had not come yet this week. He had really come to look forward to her scheduled visits. In fact, he had not had a visitor since the **40-question episode** last Monday. He realized that, while during most of the visits he actually did almost all the talking, they were very helpful to him. They gave him something to look forward to and take his mind off his condition. Also, remembering things that had happened to him, reminded him that his life up until now had been good. It had been what some might call a hard life. But even though it was a little rough, he felt he had learned some good life lessons.

When Adrian started to gasp for breath, Nurse Sally, recognizing the signs, immediately jumped into the hall, and told Nurse Kincade. Nurse Kincade grabbed the hospital speaker system and said "**Code Blue I L Room 344 Stat.**"

All staff in the hospital knew someone in room 344 had serious trouble breathing. The moment the doctor arrived, he ordered Adrian to the Iron Lung room as quickly as possible. Two big orderlies arrived at Adrian's room with a gurney. The doctor ordered Adrian taken off the IV. Adrian was quickly transferred to the gurney. His glasses were left behind.

Adrian was out of his room and barreling down the hall at breakneck speed. The orderlies, one on each side, were almost running. A doctor was sitting on the bed massaging Adrian's chest to help him breath. It was hard to explain how the doctor stayed on the bed. Perhaps lots of practice. Two more doctors and two nurses were trailing along behind.

One of the orderlies, with a booming voice kept calling out. "Make a hole! Clear the corridor!" They blasted through a couple of double doors without even slowing down. People in the corridors jumped to the side and hugged the wall.

A kitchen meal server had left a food cart in the hall, as was the custom, while she picked up the trays, after serving breakfast. She ran into the hall and grabbed the food cart. She quickly shoved it into the room she had just been in, just as the procession whizzed by.

Now the Iron Lung, or negative pressure ventilator, was the most important piece of equipment for patients who could not breathe on their own. It was designed not for beauty, but for function. At the time Adrian needed one, it was the most important piece of equipment hospitals had for people who had lost normal muscle control and needed to keep breathing. Adrian's hospital

had gotten, at this time, a total of ten. Several, sadly enough, were in use at any given time. Hopefully, patients might improve and their body take back control the function the iron lung provided. The patient could then be removed from the iron lung. Unfortunately, depending the extent of the damage polio had done, sometimes the patient was consigned to remain in an iron lung the rest of their life.

By design, the iron lung was a large cylindrical drum. The patient was slid in and out on a bed, sometimes on what was called a cookie tray, which was made to slid in and out of the cylinder, as needed. Once inside, a type of door was closed, allowing only the head and neck to remain free outside. A sealed airtight compartment, with the patient's body inside, was formed.

There were pumps that pumped in the air pressure and removed the air pressure inside the chamber, and especially the chest. The pumps were power by electric motors. Their function was usually very noisy. When the air pressure in the cylinder was pumped out and fell below the air pressure in the lungs, the lungs expanded. The lungs sucked air in from outside the patient from the room through the patients mouth and nose. air pressure in the room and outside the patient's head pushed air from outside into the lungs, through the nose and mouth, to fill up the lungs. Then, the air pressure inside the cylinder was reversed, and the air in the lungs was pushed back out of the lungs by way of the nose and mouth. This made the lungs do their job the way they were supposed to do. So, basically, the iron lung caused air to flow in and out of the lungs.

The patient had to lay flat of his back. To see anybody, he had to look up into a mirror tilted at an angle, so, he could only see someone standing behind his head. The only other thing he could see was the machinery of the iron lung itself around the head opening.

The side of the cylinder had portal windows, so attendants could reach in and adjust the body, sheets, hot or cold patches and such without opening the machine or removing the patient. There were also large, heavy glass windows to see the patient's body.

Adrian remembered seeing an iron lung once equipped with a gasoline motor. It was on a trailer being pulled down the highway behind a car with someone inside. He had asked his father what that strange thing on that trailer was. He was told it was an Iron Lung, made to load and unload off and on a trailer because the person inside could not travel without the iron lung. While it was estimated a patient could live as much as 60 years using an iron lung, most did not last anywhere near that long. At this time, the average time was about six months, depending on the lung muscles response to the help they received from the machine.

The iron lung came in one size fits all. So, the one Adrian was in, swallowed the skinny little kid he had become. He was able to only speak on the exhaled breath. This made his speech very slow and interrupted. The size of the machine, the noise, and the panic of not being able to breathe, scared the daylights out of Adrian.

Some patients who recovered from the iron lung had a fear of tight places and a dislike of sleeping on their back for years to come. Adrian believed that there were not many more scarier feelings than being paralyzed. Not being able to move your body, no matter how hard you try. Your brain will command and will your body part to move, but the muscles will just not obey. It feels like you are straining as hard as you can, but nothing is happening. That body part will not move. And when it is your lungs, real panic kicks in.

This iron lung forced Adrian to breath. The hospital had called his parents. They came as quickly as they could arrange babysitters. When his mother saw him in the iron lung the first time, she started crying. She was standing where Adrian could not see her, but he could still hear her. He managed to get out," Mother, please don't cry!"

Adrian spoke to the image of his father in the mirror over his head, "Father I am so scared. This thing frightens me. How long do I have to be in this thing?"

His father answered, "The doctors say you responded quickly to the treatment or help the iron lung is giving you. It may be big, noisy, ugly, strange machine but it is only here to help your body do what it does naturally. Why! As soon as your body gets rested up, it will take back over and do what it is supposed to do, and you can get out of this machine! Remember, it is only a machine!"

Father hoped this over simplification would make Adrian less frightened of the iron lung. Although inside, he himself was a bit overwhelmed by the size and noise of the machine. His little boy, who was down to about 75 pounds, and looked like he was nothing but skin and bones, and looked so tiny in that machine that easily could have held a grown person of 270 lbs. or more. It swallowed his son. Also, being in this room with the other iron lungs running, and doctors and nurses coming and going, in what appeared to him to be organized confusion, was not helping matters. He had been told Adrian would shortly be moved back to his room and the lung hooked up in there.

But this was not the time to give in to his own fears and concerns. He had to reassure his son and his wife. They had been through tough times before, and the Good Lord would help them through this.

"Adrian! Guess what Mother found just the other day in some old papers she was looking through? I had almost forgotten that I still had a copy of this." Father asked.

"I... don't... know," was Adrian's whispered answer.

"Well, it is a poem that I wrote when you were first born. I was so proud to have you, a son." Father bragged.

"Would you like to hear it?" Father asked.

After Adrian said yes, his father read it to him. It sounded like a great poem. Adrian was sure he liked it a lot, but it was hard to concentrate. He missed some of it due to his own labored breathing. This being made to breathing through his mouth and nose by force, was strange and uncomfortable. He had almost never even thought about breathing. He just did it without thinking, like everybody else. Of course, there were those times when he played really hard, like running a long way as hard as he could ...which was most of his running...and he had to stop and breathe really hard to catch his breath. But, as soon as he "caught his breath", he forgot all about breathing.

He also remembered those times when he would specifically think about breathing, either slow or fast that it was almost like you had to keep thinking about it and to make yourself breathe. But if you were not even thinking about breathing, you just breathed naturally with no trouble at all. It was really weird.

With struggled breath, Adrian told his parents what he remembered of the real wild ride to the iron lung.

"There was this orderly guy hollering for people to get out of the way. I saw people standing flat against the wall as we went by. Some doctor guy was pushing on my chest while as he rode on the bed thing, with me. When we came to those double doors they have here everywhere, we just busted through, without even slowing down. If I had not been so out of it, I would have really enjoyed that ride," concluded Adrian.

"You are going to be just fine," his mother said as she moved so he could see her. She ran her fingers through his hair. It was tearing her up inside to see her child so ill and small in what, to her, looked to be a big noisy and horribly frightening machine.

""The Good Lord has helped you through some real bad times before and will help you through this too. Remember that potion of several of the bible verses I like so well "it came to pass?" I believe this will come to pass also,"" Mother said, with a lot more hope than conviction.

"I put some more very pretty get-well cards in your room on a string across the top of your window. Some are also, funny. Knowing you, I am sure you will like those. We will read them to you, when you get back to your room. Also, you got some more lovely flowers. I don't know how they found out, but that Sunday School class you go to once in a while sent you some get well cards that the students signed." Mother said, also trying to change the subject from the iron lung.

"How is Lee and the **Red Headed Freckle Face** and baby Edmond?" asked Adrian. This took a long while to say on exhale breath only.

"Your brothers and sister are all fine. They all miss you a lot. But you should not call your sister, **Red Headed Freckle Face,** her name is Ann!" his mother corrected.

"But Mother, she has the prettiest red hair and cutest freckles of anybody in the whole world," Adrian said laboriously. Even in his condition he said what he thought, and not always with the most tack.

"Nevertheless, you call your sister Ann, you understand?" She said with a smile in her voice. Sick as he was, she was still his mother and would always correct him if he needed it.

"Yes Mother," he respectfully answered. Adrian said all his prayers that night but not out loud. It took just too much effort to talk. He was so glad that the **Good Lord** could hear what he was thinking. Although that idea sort od scared him at times, because he realized that his thinking was not always what he wanted anybody to hear especially the **Good Lord**.

Iron Lungs

Chapter Seventeen
Day 62: [Thur.] Polly Returns

It was a very bright sunny day outside. In fact, a ray of sunlight was now shinning right into his face. It woke Adrian up. He took a deep breath. HE TOOK A DEEP BREATH! He could breathe on his own! It came flooding back to him. He was no longer in the iron lung. He was free of his virtual prison of three weeks. They had returned him to his regular bed late last evening. That big, yellow, ugly machine just sat quietly over against one wall, waiting to be returned to its supply room. There, it would be cleaned and prepared for the next poor sole who had to make use of its services. It was great when he had needed it, and it had probably saved his life, but in all honesty, he was glad to see it go.

Adrian said, "Praise the Lord." out loud. In his mind, he was shouting, "Hallelujah! Hallelujah!" Oh Boy! Oh Boy! Oh Boy!"

That three weeks in the iron lung was probably the longest three weeks of his life, or so it seemed. One thing was for sure, he believed he would remember it forever. His active mind jumped to an earlier crisis, when he knocked himself out and woke up with both wrists wrapped up. That crises also had lasted about three weeks. What had happened was, Adrian had been playing on the playground at his school, when his family lived at the farmhouse. He was sliding down the slide with some of his playmates. Adrian always played all out. At the top of the slide, Adrian discovered that if you stood an extra step down from the top, then you jumped and pulled on the handles at the top of the slide, you could hit the slide going a lot faster than just sitting down and letting gravity pull you down.

In this incident, Adrian jumped a few times with great success. On his last jump he went sailing over the top of the slide, but he missed the slide and with both hands hanging down...the hands were positioned hanging down to grab the slides of the slide to keep from shooting out of the slide and landing on your bottom...which sometimes happened regardless, but that was just part of the fun. The next thing he remembered; he was at home with both wrists wrapped up. While he was unconscious, he had been to the doctor, got treated, and come home. Both wrists were treated, and for about three weeks, he had been wrapped in cloths and soaked in apple cider vinegar. He could never, after that, smell apple cider vinegar without remembering that **"*flying slide incident.*"**

Today it felt so good to simply breath. It was something we all take for granted until we can or do lose it. We complain about so many things and take so many things for granted. "I have complained a lot in here," was Adrian's train of thought.

Nurse Kincade had come in while Adrian was having this thought process. She sort of marveled at the smile he had on his face.

"Well Little Trooper, you look like you are in a chipper mood. You seem to always bounce back quickly.

I know that time in the iron lung was scary and very unpleasant for you. Instead of complaining you are smiling," was her observation.

Nurse Kincade notified the orderlies to come and remove the iron lung. The doctor has given instructions to leave it in the room just in case he needed to return to it.

Adrian was glad when, in less than ten minutes, the iron lung was gone. He was still paralyzed on his left side. He had the IV again. The doctors had now decided that they would give him all his medicine through the IV instead of shot in his well punctured skin. He wished they would make up their minds if they were going to use the IV or not.

When Nurse Kincade told him about the IV change he was glad. He did not really care why he was, just glad no shots, at least for a while.

It was amazing what you can be thankful for. It reminded him of his Father's quote:

"I complained because I had no shoes, until I met a man who had no feet."

His folks had been up for quick visits a couple of times while he was in the iron lung. But no visits from anyone else. He was wondering what had happened to Polly that last week, before he went to the iron lung. Not that they could have had much of a visit with everything else that was going on that night. He really missed seeing and talking to her and hoped that nothing was wrong with her. His mother had brought some papers of his father's that he had asked her to bring, so he could show them to Polly. The afternoon drug on seemingly endless. Then, when he had just about given up hope, in she walked.

She looked around and the first thing she said was, "They **told** me you were out of the iron lung."

"I wasn't until yesterday." Adrian remarked. "They got me out of it late last evening and the orderlies just removed it just a little while ago."

"Boy, I am sure glad to see you. Where were you that Thursday, not that I didn't have enough to do?" questioned Adrian.

"Well, I probably should have called the hospital and had them tell you I was not going to be here, since I know you had starting to look forward to me and my wonderful jokes. In fact, let me leave you my phone number then you can have someone call me if we miss each other. As a matter of fact, in about a month I am going to start college classes, and that will seriously limit the times I can come up here." Polly explained. "Then the last three weeks you were in the Iron Lung and they would not let me in to see you."

"It is very true that I missed <u>You</u>; The jokes, well, I am not so sure. No that is not true. As bad as they are, I do miss them also. That sounds like good news, for you, that you are going to college, but it is also bad news that I will not get to see you as much." commented Adrian.

"So, let me hear your jokes for today. No more chicken-crossing-the-road jokes, I hope." Adrian was eager, in spite of his comments.

Polly walked over to his bedside and said "Well if you can ***FACE*** them, **here** they are," said Polly with a grin:

What did one eye say to the other eye?
 Something between us smells.

What did one snowman say to the other?
Do you smell carrots.

What taste better than it smells?
The Tongue.

"There Is nothing like good jokes, and those are nothing like good jokes." Adrian ventured.

"OK then, I have two more new ones I want to try on you that are not animal jokes. However, I have found most kids like animal jokes. But here are some not animal jokes you might like. Such as.

I walked into a military surplus supply store and asked if they had any camouflage pants. "Yes, said the clerk. But we can't find them."

That beach resort was so boring and lousy, that the tide went out and refused to come back in.

Just be yourself, everybody else is taken.

"Ha! Ha! Ha! Now I liked those. They were really funny." Adrian laughed.

"By the way Polly, I had my mother bring me some things that my father wrote 'cause I don't want you to think that my father is mean, or hard, or unfeeling," Adrian said, suddenly changing the topic of conservation, as he was prone to do when an idea hit him.

"I never thought any such things about your father," Polly replied defensively.

"Polly will you bring me that folder over there on that window seat. Please?" he requested.

Adrian took the folder, after she brought it to him, and selected a worn yellowed piece of paper which hethen handed back to her. "This is a poem that my father wrote right after I was born," Adrian proclaimed, a little teary eyed.

"Let me say again, I do not think your father is mean or too hard. He has a somewhat different parenting method, a little on the strict side but not unfeeling, said Polly. "Let me read the poem."

Our Baby Boy 1936

While we were beset with
Trials of the day,
God sent a little angel to
Brighten our way.

He our consolation,
Our pride and our Joy.
This little one from Heaven
Our own Baby Boy.

When our hearts are sad
And shadows, round us fall.
We are snatched from our gloom
By his cheery little call.

Now, lest we grow weary

While we struggle to rise.
This little one was sent
Here to brighten our lives.

Your Daddy 1936

"I did not know my father had written that until very recently. Mother was going through some of his papers and found them. We move around so much that some things never get unpacked, unless they are needed right away. Before I came in here, I found a baseball glove someone had given me so long ago that it was actually too small for me. I wound up giving it to Lee," Adrian reminisced.

"Oh yeah! I have something else I want you to read but before you do, I want to assure you my dad does not drink at all, however sadly enough, there are enough uncles in the family that do. I have been told that in the country way back up in those Piney Wood, some of those old boys will drink anything and if they can't buy something, they can make it.

One story was that two of them made some whiskey that was so bad that one of the fellows held a gun on the other one to make him drink it. Then afterwards he gave the gun to his fellow and said, "now you make me drink it."

Father has seen quite a lot of what booze can do to a fellow. He heard this story somewhere and wrote it down. He then sort of added to it and filled it out a mite and came up with the funniest story I ever read. I want you to read it and in your mind's eye, picture the situation as it unfolds.

I bet you cannot read it without it sort of cracking you up." was Adrian's challenge to Polly.

"I heard Uncle Elmer say one time that good homemade piney woods whiskey would grow hair on your chest and if it set up a spell it would grow hair on the palms of your hands and the bottom of your feet. Of Course, Uncle Elmer has been known to stretch the truth a mite," Adrian remarked, mischievously.

Adrian found the paper and handed it to Polly to read. It read like this.

MY DIZZY DELIMMA

I had in the cellar of the apartment where I lived, twelve large bottles of very good whiskey. I had been keeping it for a special occasion, any special occasion. My landlady told me I had to move and take those bottles with me or else empty their contents down the sink. She told me I must get every bottle. She also told me that I needed to learn to complete a task when I started one so it had to be done that day. She also told me that drink was very bad for me and really messed me up. I told her I could and would take care of her problem.

So, I proceeded to start the unpleasant task. I would prove to her that I could finish what I started without any problem. I withdrew the cork from the first bottle and poured the contents down the sink, with the exception of one glass, which I drank. I then counted the bottles which were left, which was eleven.

I extracted the cork from the second bottle and did likewise with the contents and poured it down the sink, with the exception of one glass, which I drank. Then I counted the two corks and ten bottles which was thirteen.

I pulled the bottle from the next cork and poured the contents down the sink, except one glass full, which I drank. I counted the corks and bottles and glasses, which was fifteen.

I pulled the cork from the next glass and poured the contents down the bottle, except one drink from a glass. Next, I counted the bottles, corks, and glasses, and bottles which were nineteen.

I next pulled the bottle from the cork of the next and drank a sink full of it and threw the rest down the glass. I counted the remaining glasses, bottles, corks, and glasses and came up with twenty-two.

I finally reached the last one. I pulled the sink out of the last glass and pored the cork from the bottle. I then corked the sink with the glass and drank one cellar full. I counted the sinks and corks and glasses and bottles and one cellar that came to twenty-seven. So, I got rid of the whiskey and the sinks as the landlady told me to and finished the task in just one day.

Polly had a real good laugh over the story. "Now I see where you get your sense of humor," she chuckled.

"So, you see, I did not want you to think bad of my father. The "Bark" in his life has made him seem a little rough around the edges, but inside, he is a really loving, caring man. I think that when all us kids started coming along and he had to try to find work in the city to support all of us and to move out of his comfort zone. I heard someone use that expression, it was a big change for him. We have had to move a lot. In fact, my Father tells me that our family already has moved into the new place. When Father was younger, he wrote other poems and even a full cowboy story. I would call it a book. I don't guess anybody, but the family, ever saw them. He never got them published, only some are typed or printed up."

"You know what, my Father can play the harmonica. Every great once in a while he will get it out, and play, and sing a little while, for us kids. Man, that is a great time. It has been a while since he has done it, but I sure remember those times. I seem to be doing a lot of remembering since I have been sick and cooped up in this old hospital." reflected Adrian.

Polly understood the frustration of an active fun-loving boy like Adrian. She was not happy, however, about where his active mind went next.

"Polly, I saw a lot of iron lungs down by that room where they took me to get the one, I was in. What happened to those two kids that were down here before? I don't hear them since I came back, like I used to?" questioned Adrian, with a genuine look of concern. on his face. "The girl was Faith Miller and the guy was Freddie, something or other... a kind of foreign sounding name. Are they gone?"

"Well yes you are right they are both gone. The girl went home. She recovered from the polio virus, but it left her partially paralyzed and she will have to spend most of her time in an iron lung, probably the rest of her life. They say she may improve enough to spend a few hours out, from time to time. I suppose even that is a blessing," was Polly's sad remarks.

She did not say it out loud to Adrian, but she

thought it to herself. ""The doctors do not have a cure for polio. The treatment seems to be in a trial-and-error stage. I am sure they are doing the best they can, but so many of these kids don't make it or wind up with paralysis. I guess that is why they call it ***Infantile Paralysis***"

Polly spoke to Adrian, "The boy, Freddy Alberto Von Brawn, I really regret to say, did not made it. He passed away about three days ago." Polly informed Adrian, with a look of real sadness on her usually cheerful face. "He was really sick the whole time he was in here. I tried to cheer him up or a least talk to him several times, but he just felt too bad. He was not bitter or depressed, just plain too sick to care about much at all."

This news really saddened Adrian. Although he had never even seen these two other children, he felt a sort of connection to them. They had all been here at this end of the hospital, the first three in the county. He had even learned their names. He had spent time in an iron lung, just as they had. Yet, he was out of it now. Was he to be the next one polio would count as it's victim? Or, would he beat this thing? He sure hopped and prayed so.

Polly said it was time for her to go. She hated to leave on such a sad note but could not think of anything else to talk about. It certainly was not a time for her jokes, beside with Adrian's father's writing, they had pretty much exhausted that area of conversation. Could it be that she would have to revise her method of trying to entertain these children in the hospital?

"Good night young fellow. Don't lose my phone number, you hear?" Polly said, as she went out the door.

After Adrian said the two learned prayers he prayed.

Dear Lord I am sad about
Freddie and Faith,
I pray Freddie is up there with you.
Will you Bless Faith
And heal her completely.
Will you save Faith so
She can go to heaven with you.
Up in heaven there is
No polio or iron lungs.
Up there, she can run and play and be happy
Dear Lord, I really pray you heal me,
So, I can go home and be with my family again.
This day has been fun and sad,
I am glad you were with me all day.
I praise you Lord.
Amen

Chapter Eighteen
Day63: [Fri.] The Preacher and The Whittler

Adrian awoke with a start. He needed to go to the bathroom really bad. It took him a moment or two to remember where he was and the routine, he now had to go through in order to go to the bathroom. Oh, for the old days when you just had to crawl out of bed and go to the bathroom. Then you could come back and crawl into bed and go to sleep. Or, if you felt like it, you could stay up and do something else. Like go pester your kid brother, or sit and read, or whatever. It was the little simple things of life that you take for granted, till you no longer have them.

Adrian was not a happy camper this morning. He was having what Mother called a "pity party". That was when you start feeling very sorry for yourself, way more than is needed. She also said that it was a party that had only one guest, yourself. Lots of times, it became a sort of game when the family were all together, like at the dinner table. If one person started a **woe is me** story, the rest of the family would look at each other, then in unison, all say Oooooh! And shake their head. That usually caused the person telling the story to realize he was just feeling sorry for himself, and no one else was buying it. That's not to say that if a family member was suffering for a real injustice or hurt, then the family would rally around that member.

Adrian had another complaint this morning. It was the stupid dreams he had been having the last few nights. Unlike the angel dreams, these were like the dreams he used to have. He was always chasing someone, or someone or something is chasing him. It seemed no one ever caught anybody. Most of the time, he could not remember the details of what happened in the dream. If he did remember, what he remembered did not make much sense. If he was going to have stupid dreams, then he would rather not have dreams at all. But, how do you not dream or control your dreams? If there was a way, Adrian sure did not know it.

    While he was on a roll with complaints, which he felt hardly anyone was really interested in, he was really upset with laying down all the time. Most of the time, he had to lay on his back. If he tried laying on his left side, his left arm would, what he called, "***go to sleep***". He did not know the medical name for it. The muscles would not work, but the pinched nerves, or whatever that caused the ***going to sleep*** feeling, would tingle and let him know they did not like it. Also, all the IV tubes and such he was always attached to, got in his way of a comfortable position. Why could they at least let him set up in that big arm chair they had in his room? He was going to ask Nurse Kincade, the next time she came in, if she could arrange it somehow. He did not like being a grump or complainer, but with the ever-present pain and discomfort and with no distractions to keep his mind off them, pain made it hard to not be grumpy. He wished someone would come to see him. Polly was not due for another six days. Mother and Father were probably not going to be able to come for a few days. He had forgotten the Clergy exception. A minister or preacher could come any day like parents.

Into his room, like an answer to prayer, walked Uncle Rufus Martenson. He was sure Uncle Rufus would have some stimulating conversations and, as usual, interesting remembrances.

Uncle Rufus was a retired country Baptist Preacher. He was only retired according to the Baptist Denomination. Uncle Rufus believed that once **God** called you into the ministry of spreading the gospel, **He** never retired you. You might go about it in a different way, but the callings of God were without repentance on God's part.

Uncle Rufus knew his nephew was sick with an Illness that might very well take his life. He wanted to be sure the boy was prepared to face death. He was pretty sure the boy was saved, but that did not necessarily mean you were prepared to face death. Most people find death about the scariest thing in the world, even if everybody has to face it sooner or later.

"Well, Howdy Nephew," Uncle Rufus opened the conversation with. "Your Aunt Charlene sends her love."

"Aunt Charlene. How is she doing?" asked Adrian.

"She is fit as a fiddle," Uncle Rufus answered.

"I really appreciate Aunt Charlene," started in Adrian. "I got bunches and bunches of aunts and uncles, but she is one of my favorites. She always is so nice to me and she takes time to talk to a kid. We have had some neat conversations. When I get started, I don't know when to shut up. Also, I jump from subject to subject.

That drives some adults up a wall. She once told me that with my gift of gab, I might make a good preacher like you."

"You know those story books she gave me a while back have become some of my most prized possessions. I really love the one about the beatitudes. I looked at it, and read it so much, that I had to put tape on it to keep it together," Adrian exclaimed.

"I am sure she will be glad to hear that," Uncle Rufus commented.

"And how is your brother, Uncle Vernon?" questioned Adrian.

"You know Vernon. He is doing just fine. Right now, he is probably sitting on his front porch whittling or else working on one of his never-ending puzzles." Uncle Rufus said, with a look of exasperation on his face.

"You know, that is how I always picture him when I think of him. I don't think I can ever remember him not being on his porch whittling, when I visited him," Adrian reminisced.

"What else do you remember about Vernon?" Uncle Rufus asked. He was wise in getting a person with a sickness to think of fond memories and not of themselves and their miseries. He had spent many an hour in hospitals with the sick and knew how to prepare the conservation for unpleasant topics. Fond memories was one of them.

"Well, like everybody knows Uncle Vernon really likes to whittle. He gave me a little horse he was working on one time, it looked very real. And he also gave me my second pocketknife. Father had already given me one of his old ones, but it had a broken blade. Uncle Vernon showed me how to take care of a pocketknife. He also gave me a pocket whet stone to sharpen it with. The city kids say it is called a "wet stone", but Uncle Vernon called it a "whet stone", so that is what I always say it. That knife was what I call a handy toy and tool, it was a real beauty to me.

Mother said I could keep it because he had showed me how to take care of it. Every East Texas Country boy should have a pocketknife. In fact, any real true Texan worth his salt usually has one. They were so useful for so many things, like whittling, cutting string like on a kite, and stuff. Also, even medical emergencies like getting a splinter out of your finger."

"Uncle Vernon also taught me that a dull knife is a lot more dangerous than a sharp one. The reason being, that a sharp knife will usually cut what you want it to. A dull knife will sometimes slip or hang up then turn loose and cut you when you put pressure on it."

"I gave my old one to Lee. I also passed on the things Uncle Vernon had showed me to Lee. He can use my whet stone anytime he asks for it."

"Uncle Vernon also taught me that, not only the knife was a useful tool, it could be used in a really fun game he called **Mum-Bo-Peg.** Lee and I have played it for hours. "You open the knife on the end with two blades: the long blade straight out and the short blade halfway open. On soft ground outside, you can draw a large circle. Also, you need to decide how high you want the final score to be. The better the players, the higher final score. You balance the knife with the long blade on the round and the short blade also on the ground. This puts the handle sticking up in the air at an angle. You then hook your finger around the short blade and carefully flip the knife in the air. If it comes down with the long blade stuck into the ground, that is 15 points, and the hardest to do. If it lands as it started, with both blades touching the ground, that is 10 points. If it lands on its back, with the short blade sticking straight up, that is 5 points. Any other position than these three is a dud and counts for nothing. Also, it must land inside the circle."

The knife I gave to Lee had the third blade broken. Luckily, it was the blade at the end opposite from the long blade and worked fine for **Mum-Bo-Peg**. "I think Father broke that blade trying to use it as a screwdriver."

"When I tried to tell some of the city boys about **Mum-Bo-Peg**, one of them said that the country hicks had taken the game from a city game, called **Mumble-Peg.** He said it was played pretty much the same, except the winner drove a two-inch Peg into the ground with the handle of the knife, and the looser had to pull it out with his teeth. Because the loser would Mumble between his teeth at the winner, it was called, Mumble **Peg**. I like the country version much better."

"Besides, most of the city boys who carried knives used them mostly to threaten other kids. Also, most of them did not keep their knives in too good of a condition."

"I would show you my knife, but they would never allow it in here. Most likely they would take it away from me and I would never see it again," Adrian finished his story.

"You know what else I remember about Uncle Vernon, is his love for puzzles. I know that he, like many country people, use puzzles for entertainment. I saw several that he really liked once he finished them. He somehow put some kind of backing to hold them all together. He even put some on his walls as pictures." Adrian remembered.

Uncle Vernon said he told his two sons that they were so important to him that they were like the last piece of a puzzle. The puzzle would not be complete without the last piece. This works for any size puzzle, big or small. So, his life would not be complete without them. So, sometimes he would call them his **Last Piece Kids**. I think that is neat," Adrian stated.

Uncle Rufus said, "I agree with you that Vernon is really into puzzles. He is quite predictable in many ways."

"I'll say, he is predictable. He is one of those people that I call a **Broken Record Response** person," Adrian exclaimed.

"Now what do you mean by that?" questioned Uncle Rufus scratching his head.

""Well, every time anyone ask him what he is going to do or when he is going to do something, he says ***I don't have to do anything, but pay taxes and go when the Old Master calls me.*** I know I have heard him say it a hundred times. I think Father asks him what he is going to do just to hear him say it,"" Adrian recounted.

"You know, when you think about it, country folks have a lot of sayings that they all know what they mean, like when they intend to do something, they will say: ***If***

the Good Lord's willing, and the creek don't rise! You hear that one over and over. Or, when you ask them how they are feeling they often answer you with, **Fair to Middling.** They say it every time, like a broken record. That is not a criticism. It is just something I noticed. In fact, I do it to." Mother has a saying; I don't have any idea where she learned it. It makes no sense to me. Also, I don't think she means it, at least I hope she does not. When she wants you to do a special favor for her, she will say If ***you will do this, I will dance at your wedding with a cow bell on.*** That really, really makes no sense I can understand. Why would anyone want to dance with a cow bell on?"

"We had a land lord in the city once, that every time you asked him how he was doing, he always said, ***I never felt better, had less, and needed more in my whole life*** He said it every time. No matter how many people asked or how often. We kids memorized it, and I am ashamed to say, we mimicked him when his name came up in our conversations."

"That reminds me. Have you ever noticed how people will ask each other when they meet, how are You? The other person will answer, Fine thank you. And neither person really expects a truthful answer to the question or the answer. I like to surprise people once in a while and truthfully answer the question with something like, I feel lousy. Or, "Now that you asked, I am in a bad mood today." Or I say "You don't want to know."

"You will be surprised the shock they have that you really answered the courtesy question that they did not expect an answer. I am ashamed that I do it sometimes just to shake people up."

Oh, I almost forgot, I have something for you that your Uncle Vernon made especially for you. I know you have heard people say that they would do such and such when they got around to it. Well your Uncle Vernon thought he would help you never be caught in such a situation. It is a wafer like section cut from a tree limb. On one side he carved the letters I and T on the other side he carved the letters T and U. So, looking at as a whole you have a round TU on one side and IT on the other, so a round Tu It.

After he stopped laughing Adrian said. "That is so funny and very clever."

At this time, Nurse Kincade came into the room. Adrian asked her if Uncle Rufus could put him in the armchair. She said it would be okay, instead having to call for orderlies. Uncle Rufus easily lifted Adrian and put him into the chair. He was now so small that they had to put lots of pillows on each side of him so he would not fall over.

"Talk of an overstuffed chair this is ridicules," joked Adrian, about himself.

"I hope you will be comfortable there. If you are not, I can put you back anytime you say," Uncle Rufus stated.

Uncle Rufus, in an attempt to get the conservation somewhere near back on track so he could talk about what he came to talk about, mentioned that he was glad when he recalled the time Adrian's family had come to his church.

"Yeah, I sure enjoyed coming to that church. Some

real good preaching and I especially liked the **Dinner on the Grounds."**

Adrian's mind took another "bunny trail."

"One time, when we had all that good food, I was hurrying through the line to get to the good stuff, like pies and cake. I knew I had to get a few vegetables to make it look good, but I really hated English peas. When I got to the lady passing out the English peas, I tried to skip her, but she reached out took my plate and loaded it down with English Peas. I had been taught to not waste food and clean up my plate. The peas lady had hardly left me room for anything else. I then had a great idea. I would eat all those peas then have room for the good stuff. So, I got out of line, sit down next to a tree, and quickly gulped down all those peas."

""I then got back in line right past the pea lady. However, she spotted me. She reached over and grabbed my plate again. She said to the lady next to her. "Bless his little heart. Look, he as eaten all the peas I gave him. He loves them so much; I am going to give him some more." Then she dumped another large helping of peas on my plate. I tell you; I was so mad that I got out of line again, went behind a large tree and dumped those peas on the ground, waste or not. I reentered the line way down from the pea lady.""

"Well eating was not all we did at those, *dinner on the grounds*," suggested Uncle Rufus.

"Oh no, we also played fun games. The young guys usually got up a ball game, and the older men played horse shoes or washers: a similar game, only with a hole at each end, and using large washers to toss into the hole. Some of the kids played chasing games." Adrian remembered.

"Then, coming on dark, someone would bring out a guitar or a fiddle, and sometimes an accordion or a harmonica, or all of these. And then we would have us a singing. There is nothing like good old country gospel music. Once in a while, some of the men would do a quartet. That was <u>living</u> church in the fullest." Adrian stopped to catch his breath.

"Are you comfortable in your standing with Jesus?" Uncle Rufus asked.

"Absolutely, I gave my heart to Jesus years ago. I know he watches over me and hears and answers my prayers. I really hate being in this hospital and having polio, but I don't believe Jesus did it to me. I just happened to be one of the many kids that got it this year. I do believe that Jesus can heal me and make me well again," Adrian stated emphatically.

"Adrian I also believe Jesus can and will heal you, but just suppose he decides not to. What then? If he decides to take you to heaven, how do you feel about that?" Uncle Rufus asked.

"Well, I really hope that does not happen just yet. Heaven is a really great place from all I have been taught.

So, I guess if I have to, it will not be so bad, except for my family I would have to leave behind. I don't really want to go for a long time. I would like to live to be an old man with lots of kids and grandkids. But I know everybody will have to go someday, right?" Adrian asked seriously. "I sure don't want to go to that other place."

Adrian's skip subject mind kicked in, all of a sudden and he said ""Uncle Rufus, I remember a story I heard about Heaven."

Without waiting for a response, Adrian jumped into story telling mode. """There was this rich fellow that really loved being rich. He was a Godly man, believed in Jesus, he gave to the poor, and did charitable works. but he had one hang-up. He dreaded being poor more than anything else. When he got old, and was about to die, he sold all he had and converted it into two solid Gold Bricks. When he died, he met St. Peter at the Pearly Gates with a carpet bag that contained the two Bricks of Gold. St. Peter told him that "You cannot take anything into heaven with you." The man explained that what he had in the bag represented a lifetime of work and effort. He tried to explain how useful what he had in the bag could be. St. Peter told him again "You cannot bring anything with you. Nevertheless, let me see what you think is so important" The man opened his bag and showed St. Peter the Gold Bricks.""

St. Peter exclaimed, "Look around you man, You brought <u>Pavement</u>?"

Uncle Rufus got a real kick out of that story. He thought that although it was a funny joke, it also had some good points that would make sound preaching. But after a short pause, he tried to get the conservation back on the purpose of his visit.

"What do you think death is?" he rather abruptly asked.

"Well, I guess it is when you stop living," Adrian said.

"Let me tell you, it is simply when you...the real You...stops living in one body, it goes into another body. The big question is where that next body is going to spend the rest of time. If you have accepted Jesus as your Savior, it is in Heaven. If you have not accepted Jesus, the you will spend it in a terrible place, called Hell. There are no other options," Uncle Rufus explained.

"If you believe there is a **God**, then you must also believe that **He** knows what **He** is doing. If he did not know what **He** was doing, and was perfect at it **He** would not be **God**. **He** gave us the Bible, and lots of preachers, and in the old days, prophets, and teachers, to tell us what **He** decided to do with us and how he was going to do it. It really does not matter if we don't understand it, or would like it another way, or even believe it. **His** way is the only way. **He** gave man a right to make a choice to do it **His** way or not. then sent **ONE** answer for that choice. You don't have to believe it, or even like it, but that is the way it is. It does not depend on if you believe or not. People may think that this is not fair, but we must remember that **God** is absolutely just. What we think is fair is based on our understanding and opinions not God's. **He** only does what is right."

"Also, **He** is not only a God that just loves. **He** is **<u>Love</u>**. Everything **He** does is because **He** is Just and **He** loves us. And **He** knows what **He** is doing," Uncle Rufus declared.

"Wow! Said that way, does not leave man any wiggle room," Adrian declared.

"Well! You are right. Salvation, Life, and Death are serious subjects that deserve serious thought. We don't need to be afraid of them, but they do need to be settled in our mind. And, it is best to confront them ahead of time instead of in a time of crisis. If our response and understanding is settled ahead of time, then death and such are not near so scary." Uncle Rufus said.

"You know, boy, when you get a preacher wound up, he just naturally starts preaching," Uncle Rufus apologized.

"Uncle Rufus I would expect nothing less from you. I am really glad you came by today. I was hoping earlier today someone would show up. So, I guess the Good Lord picked you." Adrian replied. "Therefore, I guess I needed to hear it."

"Also, I wonder if you could put me back in bed, please?" Adrian asked.

"I will be glad to, Son," Uncle Rufus replied. "I did not mean to wear you out."

"Oh no! As I said, you were an answer to my prayer. I was desperate for some company. And there is no telling when Nurse Kincade could have gotten the orderlies back up here to move me, as it was a request, not a medical emergency." Adrian said, sort of breathlessly.

Despite Adrian's protest, Uncle Rufus realized the sitting up had tired Adrian out. He also realized that he had accomplished his task of speaking to Adrian about death, albeit, in not as smooth a conservation as he would have liked.

"I suppose I should be shoving off. I am praying it is the Lord's will, that you are healed and get out of here real soon," exclaimed Uncle Rufus.

"Well, I am glad a preacher is praying for me as well, 'cause I need all the prayer I can get," Adrian exclaimed.

"Well, being a preacher does not make my prayers any more important than anyone else. **God** looks on the heart and the faith and the sincerity of those doing the praying." Uncle Rufus explained.

"**God** hears <u>all the prayers</u> of <u>all his children</u>. And, while I am on the subject of answered prayer, you need to realize that there are three answer to prayers. There is Yes, which is the one we like best. Then there is No. We don't like that one, but **God** always has a reason for saying No. **He** may not share it with you, but be assured, **He** has a good reason. And remember, **He** does not have to explain **Himself. He** is **God**. And lastly, **God** can say Not Now, Maybe Later. This means that certain things have to happen before the answer can come. Most of us don't like this one either. However, we can be sure of one thing: **God** will always answer correctly, like it or not. **He** is just. Because **He** is perfect. Boy! You got me to preaching again," exclaimed Uncle Rufus.

"Ha, Ha, I know you can't help it. It is who you are. But it is good preaching," Adrian said chuckling.

"Well, I am fixing to hit the road, I need to be on my way," Uncle Rufus said as he rose to go. I'll come see you again ***The Good Lord willing and the creek don't rise.*** Oh no I did it didn't I?"

"Ha, Ha, give my love to Aunt Charlene and say Howdy to Uncle Vernon next time you see him," Adrian asked as Uncle Rufus left.

"Will do," said Uncle Rufus with a wave as he

exited the door.
    That night Adrian prayed.

That was quite a visit, Lord.
You done gave me,
A lot to think about.
You also reminded me,
Of some good stuff.
I am going to keep on,
Asking You to heal me,
And get me out of this Hospital.
Please forgive me all my Sins.
I am truly sorry Lord
Please make me a better boy.
Please bless Mother and Father,
And Lee, Ann, and Edmond.
Also please bless all my,
Uncles and Aunts,
Especially, Aunt Charlene
And Uncle Rufus.
Also, my whittling uncle
Uncle Vernon.
Please forgive me all my sins
Sorry done said that.
And bad thoughts.
Amen.

Start Position   **15 Points**

10 Points   **5 Points**

Chapter Nineteen
Day 67: [Tues.] The Death Revelation

Adrian's woke when he tried to turn over on his left side and could not. His brain had forgot the message that his left side would not do what it was told. The struggle ended when, once awake, he remembered his left side was paralyzed. This was a real bummer. He remembered that when he first came into the hospital, he was complaining that he could not get up and run and play. Now he could not even turn over in bed. He realized how much we ought to be thankful for, that which we are able to do, instead of complaining about what we cannot do. We should pray that **God** will help us to do better and be more thankful.

One of father's jokes popped into Adrian's head. It was **"They told me to cheer up, things could be worse. So, I cheered up, and sure enough, things got worse."**

Shortly after they brought in what they called breakfast, which he could not understand why, since he had been on intravenous feeding for a while, the doctor's arrived. "Dr. B and The Shadow." They did their thing of poking, and examining him top to bottom, to discover what he could move and what he could not. They took his temperature again, although the nurse had taken it just 30 minutes before and wrote it on his chart. Adrian thought their examination made him feel like that deer he had seen that one of his uncles had shot, then hung in a tree, before he skinned it, and decided how to cut it up.

Dr. Billings said to Dr. Jones, on completion of the examination. "I believe we are going to lose this one. We have done all we can, and nothing we try seems to stop the progress of the virus. Emotionally, he has kept up his spirits. Medically, I don't understand it, but his sort of irrational sense of humor, and his faith in God, have mentally keep him from dwelling on his illness and condition. It has actually helped him, but not enough. We get all kinds with this polio, but few like him. Sure, we try as hard as we can. And it is a shame to lose any, but I believe this one will not make it more than two weeks at the rate he is going. Our best bet is to keep him on strong pain killers so as to make him as comfortable as possible for the time he has left."

Dr. Jones said, "I can only say that I agree with your assessment of the situation, Doctor. I hope someone will someday come up with a vaccine that can stop this terrible virus. That would be an untold blessing to mankind."

Dr. Billings continued. Sometimes he seemed to ignore even Dr. Jones. "As you know, we got three more cases of polio just yesterday, one of which had to go right into an iron lung. That makes our total of polio cases up to twenty-three now. With our other case load, I think we are going to need to have more doctors brought in to handle what is turning to another epidemic as bad as last year. Which one do you suggest we look in on next?"

Dr. Jones said, "Well the girl in....."

That was all Adrian heard as they left out into the hall. "I can't believe it, they just said I was going to be dead in two weeks," he screamed in his mind. "That can't be true! I just know that the Good Lord is going to heal me somehow! Sure, I am really sick, and paralyzed, and everything, but that is no problem for Jesus. He can do anything."

Adrian's thoughts skipped to his second great passion "family". Here he was up here, in this hospital, with mostly strangers. He wanted to see his brothers and sister. He wanted to see more of his Mother and Father, and not just for a few minutes. And not only ever once in a while, when they could get away. They had to drive all the way up here to the hospital just to visit him. It was not near enough. "I have got to talk to my Father about this," he thought.

Adrian thought about what the doctors said, all day.

Later, when Mother and Father came, it was the first thing Adrian said to them. "Father, the doctors say I am going to die in two weeks!"

"Son, are you sure that is what they said?" Father asked, in disbelief. "Tell me just exactly what happened."

"Well, they came in this morning and started all that examination stuff, like they always do. Then Dr. Billings said that they were going to lose this one meaning me. I thought, at first that maybe they meant something else. But then he said it again, and added that I would probably not make it more than two weeks. Father, does that mean they think I will not live more than two weeks?' asked Adrian, tearfully.

He had not cried all day while he thought about it, but now telling it to his father and mother, made him feel just awful. Not only for himself, but also for them, when he saw the looks on their faces. His mother turned away and started to cry softly. After a moment, mixed with shaken feelings and concern, his father started to get angry.

"Son, I am going to get to the bottom of this right now. They should never be saying such things right in front of you, even if they believe it is true." said Adrian's father.

"Now Honey! Don't you go blowing off the handle till you talk to them and get all the facts," mother cautioned Adrian' father. "Calm down a minute, then go ask them if it is true. You know when you go off halfcocked, you usually only make matters worse."

"I am calm! I am calm!" Father protested. He was not, and realized that Mother was right. He sat down in a chair for about five minutes while no body said a word, then he got up and left the room quickly, without another comment.

All mother could say was, "Oh my!"

Adrian knew better than to say anything to his father at that time.

Adrian's father walked down the hall purposefully, and quickly, jerked open Dr. Billing's office door, and walked right in. Dr. Billings looked up from the stack of papers on his desk with a surprised look at the interruption. He almost knocked over the half-empty cup of coffee onto the half-eaten sandwich he had started some hours ago.

Dr. Jones fell over backward in the chair he had been leaning back on its two back legs. "What is the meaning of this? You can't just come busting in here like this" he said after he got up off the floor.

"I can, and I did," Father said. "I want to know what you said in front of my son, and if you did say what he says you said, why in the world would you say it in front of him?"

Dr. Billings who was not really an unfeeling, or unkind man, started to apologize.

Dr. Jones spoke up, and started to defend Dr. Billing. "Just what do you think that Dr. Billings allegedly said?"

Father started to heat up again, "You shut up! I am talking to him!"

Again, Dr. Billings started to apologize. "It is all my fault. I get so wrapped up in my diagnosis, that I sometimes forget that the patient is hearing what I am discussing with my colleague. He pointed at the red-faced Dr. Jones."

Father was not a little man and looked more than a little agitated.

Dr. Billings eyed Father as he continued, "I apologize very profusely for my lack of inattentiveness. However, what I said was my diagnosis, and as much as I regret it, I stand by it."

"You mean you are giving up on my son! I brought him here for you to cure him and make him well not to treat him as some kind of experiment that you work on, then give up on when you run out of thing you know to do," Father said, in frustration!

"I am truly sorry, but we truly do not know anything else to do. Until someone comes up with a vaccine for Poliomyelitis that is a workable cure, we can only try what we know. There are thousands of cases nationwide. They are all in the same boat as we are. Research scientist say we are as much as ten or twelve years away from a working vaccine. Until such a time as that happens, we can only struggle along and do the best we can with what we do know," Dr. Billings recited, with a sigh. Your son is not responding to any treatment and is and will get steadily worse. It has been our experience at the stage he is at right now, the patients go down fast, usually in about two weeks. We can and will give him Morphine. It is the standard painkiller we use, so he basically will feel little or no pain or trauma. I know this is not the answer that you or any parent wants to hear. Sadly, it is the only answer I have. I guess that I have allowed myself to become very over worked with a near hopeless problem. I confess that I concentrate more on the problem than the patient. I was hoping Dr. Jones there would help me in that area. Such does not seem to be the case," explained Dr. Billings.

Dr. Jones squirmed in his seat and looked as if he would rather be any other place than in that room at that moment.

Father had cooled down considerable at the doctor's explanation. It is a good thing that Dr. Jones had the sense to be quite when he did. He came very close to being involved in an incident that both he and Father would have regretted at a later date.

Dr. Jones admired Dr. Billings tremendously, which, in and of itself, was alright. However, idol worship can get you into a lot of trouble if it allows you to lose prospective of the world around you. He was young and good looking and would have been a hit with the young nurses, if it had not been his obvious fascination with Dr. Billings and his work. Father would say "**He shot himself in the foot**."

Father hurried back to Adrian's room, remembering that he had left Mother rather abruptly. He knew her well enough to know she would be worried that his temper could get him into some trouble. It would not be the first time and perhaps not the last.

The first thing he said to her as he reentered the room was, "Don't worry, Dear I did not do anything rash, although I sure felt like it when I left this room. I had a heart to heart with Dr. Billings. He explained why he said what he did and apologized for how and where he said it."

"Now that mealy mouth Dr. Jones and I were about to go to fist city, if he had not had the sense to shut up when I told him to," Father commented.

Always the peacemaker, Mother asked, "So, did he say what Adrian thinks he did?"

"Well, I am afraid so. He actually admitted that he did say he thinks that Adrian will probably be dead within two weeks. They think they have done all they can for him." Father said, as he took Mother, who had started to cry and shake with the emotion of her sobs, into his arms.

"Please don't cry, Mother. I am not dead yet." Adrian pleaded.

"No, you are not son! No, you are not! I pray the Good Lord will not let my son die," was the condolence of Mother.

Adrian came to a decision which he had been turning over in his mind and debating with himself all day, since the doctors had made their dreaded statement.

"Mother! Daddy! I believe that the Good Lord is going to make me well, **but** if not, then I want to die at home with my family," was Adrian's declaration, which he made as emphatic as he was able.

Father was not sure he heard what his son had said because he was holding his sobbing wife. "What was that? What did you just say son?"

"I have been thinking about it all day. The doctors have given up doctoring me. They think I am going to die in two weeks. They said so to each other and now to you. I believe the Good Lord is going to make me well and heal me completely. But if **He** decides not to, and I am going to die anyway, I want to die at home, with my family," was the speech Adrian had been rehearsing in his mind most of the day.

His parents just looked at each other for a moment. This announcement took them by surprise. Father had recently said that this time in the hospital, short as it had been, had a maturing effect on his son. He had lost a lot physically, but seemed to gain emotionally as well. A sort of maturating. He had faced his giant and stared him down.

His reasoning sort of took his parents back. They looked at each other, then Father said, "We will be right back," and they went out into the hall to talk. Knowing Adrian's hearing, they did not dare discuss things where his hearing might pick up their conversation. After what seemed a long time to Adrian, they came back into his room. Father not only lost his temper quickly, but he also made decisions quickly.

"Son," he said, "You want to go home! You are going home!"

"Are you really, really, sure this is the right thing to do, Dear?" Mother asked, one last time.

"I have listened to what my son has said, and it makes sense. Furthermore, I agree with him. I don't believe this place can do him any more good. They, themselves, have admitted it. I believe it is high time we put this totally in God's hands...live or die. Besides, after that stunt they pulled of discussing his life or death, right in front of him, still has me steamed. I no longer trust them with my son," Father said, raising his voice, and waving his arms with emotion. "I believe like Adrian. They confess they can't heal him, while he and we believe **God** can. If not, then he should pass with family close by, not in some hospital room with strangers."

"Well Dear, if you believe this is the right thing to do, then I agree with you and will back you all the way," declared Mother. Once she was convinced her husband was right, she backed her man come hell or high water.

Father pulled out his Illinois Railroad pocket watch, a gift from his father to remind him of his railroad days...Father had carried it for years...and studied it for a few moments, deep in thought.

Adrian could tell that Father was deep in thought, from the look on his face. Father was a man of action, but his hard life had thought him it is best to have a plan of operation ready before rushing into things blindly. He figured that getting Adrian out of this County Hospital might not be as easy as getting him in.

Having a plan in mind, Father turned to Adrian and said, "Son, your Mother and I have some arrangements and things to fix at home before we get you out of here. We must go home and do some things and rearrange some things before we can take you home. We will be back for you tomorrow at about three pm. You watch for us. Can you be patient and make out till then?"

"Yes Sir!" declared Adrian.

"You keep looking for us because we **Will** be here. But don't say anything about this to anybody 'till we come to get you," Father warned.

"Yes Sir!" Adrian said again, with a little bit of a conspiratorial tone in his voice.

Mother added, "You will like our new house. I will fix you up a place just for you. When you get well, there are some nice children in the neighborhood you and Lee can play with. We were able to rent in a nice quiet and peaceful neighborhood."

Adrian thought that was so like his mother. She, in her mind, already had him well and playing with kids in the neighborhood. She was always optimistic, always looking forward to better times, and circumstances. It was her way of dealing with the often harshness of her life and that of her family. In her mind, **God** was always faithful, and things were always going to get better. She lived her faith instead of giving lip service to it.

After hugs and a few more tears from his mother, Adrian's parents said goodbye and left.

Adrian had mixed emotions along with his ever-present pain. He was excited about the secret plan to spring him from the hospital. He was trying as best he could to exercise the faith that **God** was going to heal him, no matter what the doctors said, or his weakened, non-functioning, body manifested. What would the new house be like? What would it be like seeing his siblings again after what seemed like months and months?

His prayer was,

> *Dear Lord I know that you know,*
> *What we have been talking about tonight.*
> *Please, please, make me git well.*
> *Could you do it really quick?*
> *Please help my father get me out,*
> *Of this old hospital tomorrow.*
> *Help my mother,*
> *Not to cry and feel so bad.*
> *Please bless Lee, Ann, and Edward*
> *And everyone in my family*
> *Including all my many Aunts*
> *And Uncles and Cousins*
> *And Polly the Candy Stripper.*
> *All the kids and even The Adults*
> *In this Hospital*
> *Amen!*

Chapter Twenty
Day 68: [Wed.] The Signing, Going Home

Adrian woke with a start. This was the day he would make his escape. The plan was shrouded in secrecy. His body tingled, was it excitement, or just another weird manifestation of his constant companion of late: pain? He had, had a bad night. He kept waking up. He had almost knocked over the urinal, which would have been another disaster he would have had to face. He finally raised a nurse to come empty it. This had been a night problem that had happened before, as the night nurses were not near as attentive as those during the day. What a gross thing to wake up having to think about. He knew it was going to be a long day. Time always passed so slow when you are waiting for something.

He felt hungry, but nothing they brought him was easy to get down. Nurse Kincade said that was because the muscles in his throat on the left side were partially paralyzed. There ought to be something he could swallow. He felt if he could just think of it, then get them to give it to him, he could probably get it down. They, of course, had all their rules and procedures they had to abide by, so going outside the box was not going to happen. They did give him, out of desperation, a little orange juice, even if it tended to give him that rash.

About noon, Adrian asked Nurse Kincade if she would rearrange his room by moving the guest chair and putting his bed over under the window.

She said, "Why not? This kid deserves all the breaks he can get. I am the head nurse on this floor and, if I want to bend the rules a bit, nobody had better try to stop me or get in my way. She also knew about the doctor's insensitive proclamation, and disapproved of it. She believed that the main part of her duty was to see to the wellbeing and comfort of the patients, to the best of her ability. She constantly stressed this to those nurses who had to serve under her. Many a young nurse had her ears pined back for lack of compassion to the patient under their care.

After a couple of hours, by the clock, Adrian decided he would put his plan into motion. The side rails were up on both sides of his bed so he would not roll off the bed on to the floor. Should that happen, they knew he did not have the strength to get back into the bed. His left side was next to the window. With his right hand, he reached across his chest and grasped the left rail. With strength born of desperation, and which he did not know he had, he pulled himself up and lay his face on the window sill. By looking sideways, he could see down into the hospital parking lot below. He watched the cars coming and going. He tried to pick out his parent's car from the topside view. Of course, he had never seen the top of the car, but maybe he could see them get out of the car. It was a gamble born of anxiousness and hope.

When he heard someone coming down the hall that might just be coming into his room, he simply released his grip with his right hand and flopped back into the bed on his back. He did this over and over for about thirty minutes.

Finally, he had no strength left and had to give it up.

Adrian's parents showed up finally. Mother had brought Adrian some clothes. Mother, for a reason she could not explain, had picked them up at a thrift store two days before, not knowing at the time Adrian would be coming home so soon. These were to replace his old clothes they were told to burn earlier. They happened to be Brown Corduroy. Sort of a "Up Town" look to Adrian. It was all the Thrift Store had in the size she wanted. She had purchased the size he wore before he went to the hospital, but he had loss so much weight that they were several sizes too big for him. Mother proceeded to put the clothes on Adrian, even though they were too big for him. The tennis shoes were so big, that there was no way they would stay on his feet. She decided to put his shoes back in her bag and let Adrian wear the heavy socks that the hospital furnished. She took down the cards he had received, and she had put over his window and put those in the bag she had brought. She made sure to get his glasses and his Round Tu It. The flowers, she decided to leave.

Earlier that morning Mother had called Aunt Stella May and asked her to keep the kids a day or two except for baby Edmond. They would pick him up after Adrian got home. She and Father had told them what they planned to do. Aunt Stella May and Uncle John Boy were not too sure that it was the right thing to do, but they were family and would give what support they could. Father had gone somewhere and picked up a small single bed with a mattress and side rails. They had set it up in the living room, which would double as Adrian's bedroom for the time being.

While mother was dressing Adrian, Father had gone to check Adrian out of the hospital. "We are taking my son out of the hospital. He is Adrian North, in room 344. Let me sign whatever papers I need to sign, in order to do that," Father demanded, not too gently.

The discharge clerk looked up the name and said, "We can't do that! **You can't do that! He has not been discharged.**"

"Oh yes you can! And, oh yes I can!" Father said rather loudly. He was starting to get heated up.

The nurse called for the doctor and security. They both showed up quickly. When Dr. Billings showed up, he told security it was okay and he would handle it.

"Mr. North, what seems to be the trouble?" the doctor questioned.

"The problem is that I want to check my son out of this hospital and take him home, and this clerk person will not give me the papers to do that," Father said, loudly.

"Now, Mr. North, you don't want to get angry," cautioned Dr. Billings.

"Angry? You want to see angry? If you don't get those papers up here right away, you are going to really see angry," Father threatened. What no one present realized that they were dealing with a nephew twice removed of Big Bubba.

Dr. Billings turned to the clerk and said, "Give him discharge papers F1 through F3, as well as a B-26."

"A B-26?" she questioned. "I have never had one

216

of those before." Nevertheless, she produced it.

Turning to Father, Dr. Billings said, in his most condescending voice, as if he were talking to someone who was not fully in possession of his or her faculties, "You remember we told you your son will be dead within two weeks. If you insist in removing him from this hospital, and he then dies, as he will, you and your wife must both sign this form. It states that you release this hospital, and all doctors and persons connected with the hospital, from any liability in your son's death. You will not sue, are in any way, blame the hospital or its staff for his death. Nor can you bring him back and try to check him in."

"Give me all those papers. I will sign them right now," Father said, as he reached for the papers.

"I am afraid your wife will have to sign them also," reminded Dr. Billings.

"I heard you the first time!. You wait right here. I am going to get my son and my wife and she will sign your papers on our way out of this place." Father stated, and without waiting for a reply, he turned and headed for Adrian's room.

Father walked back to Adrian's room and picked up his son out of the hospital bed. Mother, carrying her bag with Adrian's stuff, followed along behind him.

Nurse Kincade had heard what was going on and come in and told "Little Trooper" goodbye. She had also given mother a fresh bedpan and urinal and some soap and creams and pain pills, they had been using on Adrian, to go in mother's bag.

Father noticed how light Adrian's 70 pounds were,

compared to the boy he had carried into the hospital just a few short weeks ago.

"You have to also sign some papers at the desk, Dear," Father said as they left the room for the last time. They stopped briefly at the desk, and Mother signed the papers and stuffed their copies into her bag.

Adrian noticed as they waited and then got on the elevators and the doors closed behind them, that all the doctors and nurses in sight were sadly shaking their heads.

In the parking lot, Mother got in the back seat of the car. Father put Adrian in gently, on some soft blankets they had thoughtfully brought with them, and arranged him, so his head was in his mother's lap. She, out of habit, began to run her fingers through his hair. She spoke softly and lovingly to him, as only a mother can do. Adrian did not even notice the ever-present pain he usually had.

Their new house was located in a very nice neighborhood. Mother had raised Adrian up so he could see it as they passed through. The streets were clean, and the yards were green. Nice, old, trees lined the sidewalks and streets. You could tell that the developer of that neighborhood had used mostly three versions of the same floor plan. Most of the houses were using the very popular siding of asbestos slate shingles. Also, most had garages that were not connected to the house. Adrian did not see a Peavey-kept type yard in the lot.

Due to the hour, most of the folks had gone in for the evening. You could hear a radio or two playing through open windows as you passed by the houses.

Mother said, "That one is our house, Son," She pointed out a nice brown house as Father turned into the driveway covered with shells. A lot of driveways in Houston had used crushed oyster shells. Adrian remembered that before Polio his feet were so tough on the bottom that it hardly hurt to walk on a shell driveway. He sadly knew that was no longer the case, after those few weeks in the hospital. His wandering mind jumped to how often he had to be instructed to wash his feet by his mother before he got into bed, in times past.

While they did not have to take a bath every night in his family, like many folks, but those feet were usually a most necessary chore. He could not wait 'till he had cause to do that chore again, because he had been running and playing barefoot. Father parked the car and came back to pick him up and carry him into the house.

"I am going to get well real soon and you won't have to carry me anymore, Father," Adrian bravely said.

"I know that is right," Father said, in a broken voice.

Adrian though, that compared to the hospital or even the old motel, this would be a much better place to die, if it came to that.

Adrian was settled into the living room that would be almost his own for the time being. His mother told him that his father had bought the small bed with side rails just that morning. What Adrian was most excited about was the pajamas! No longer a hospital gown. No longer even the too big street clothes, as welcome as they had been. The pajamas looked brand new.

Adrian said to his mother, "I love these pajamas,

Mother. They look brand new. Are they?"

"Well, yes and no. You see I bought them last week at a yard sale for a dime. The lady who was selling them had bought them for her grandson who was supposed to come for a visit. Something happened, and his visit was postponed, and he could not come for a year, and by that time, he had grown too big for them, and she could not take them back. She had never even taken them out of the package. So, you see, they are both new and old," explained Mother. "So, do you still like them as much?

"Like them? I love them!" was his answer. He was learning to better appreciate the little things in life. He was ecstatic over a year-old pair of practical new, pair of pajamas, that were bought for a dime.

Adrian looked serious for a moment and said, "Mother, can I change the subject?"

"Somehow I thought that sooner or later you might," Mother said, with a smile.

"Mother, as much as I hate them, do you have a bedpan and urinal handy? I still can't walk, but I need them really bad right now."

"I never know where the conservation is going to go when I talk to you. But, in answer to your question, yes, we do have a bedpan and urinal. In fact, thanks to Nurse Kincade, we have a brand new, unused set. She presented them to me that last minute, just before we left your room. I am pretty sure she had taken a liking to you." was Mother's reply with a twinkle I her eye.

"Well, she always did call me **Little Trooper**," commented Adrian.

Mother fetched the equipment, and they quickly

took care of Adrian's need. No sooner than they had solved that problem than Adrian thought of another problem. If his so-called bedroom was so public, how was he going to take care of this kind of business with his siblings and other people running all over the house? This was not like the hospital room, where the nurses paid no attention to it, as it was just part of their routine, and guest could be asked to step out into the hall. He voiced this problem to Mother.

"You do come up with the strangest worries," Mother said, shaking her head. "We will take care of it. We will assure that you have your privacy. Folks can be sent into the other parts of the house, including the kids."

"Mother, I have another problem," Adrian began.

"Why am I not surprised," Mother said with a chuckle in her voice.

"I am hungry," Adrian stated. "What I would really like is some buttermilk. They would not give me any in the hospital."

Things had been happening so fast that Mother had not thought how or what they were going to do about feeding Adrian.

"Buttermilk? Let me check with your Father. I will be back in a few minutes?" Mother said, as she hurried out of the room.

She found Father busy with something in the back of the house. "We did not think about feeding Adrian," was her opening comment. "You know the hospital has had a hard time trying to get him to take anything here lately. He is asking for buttermilk."

"You are right, we did not think about feeding him.

I guess I was still thinking of him as that kid I never could get full. Well, if he wants buttermilk, give him buttermilk."

"You do have some, right?" Father asked.

"Well yes! I have two new quarts I bought just yesterday in the icebox. You know, it does not last long around here. We all drink it, except Ann, she always says she can't stand it, as you know. And of course the baby," Mother answered.

"You sure it will be alright? The hospital never would try it." She asked.

"That bunch doesn't know everything. They gave up on him, remember? If he thinks he can drink it, then let him have it. It just might be good for him. As far as I know, he has not asked for anything in the way of food or drink, except orange juice since, he went in there," reasoned Father. "He is of good country stock, and country folks have good instincts."

Mother was not sure if a lot of that was just country bragging, but the bottom line was her husband approved of giving Adrian buttermilk. She opened a quart and put it in a glass with a straw. She took it back to Adrian and let him sip it. She had to hold up his head. He took several fairly good sips before he stopped.

"Could you just leave it here and give me some more in a little while?" he pleaded.

"Of course," Mother assured him.

"Mother, Grandma Rose does not have a cow anymore, does she?"

"Well, you know she does not," Mother answered! "Why do you ask?"

"I seem to remember when I was really little, that we went to Grandma Rose's and she had a cow, and she was often churning milk in a great big churn. I seem to remember that she let me help a little, but it was kind of hard. And afterward, she gave me some fresh-made buttermilk. It was the best buttermilk I have ever tasted. Better even than what you can buy in the store now. Mother, do you remember a cow and a churn?" Adrian asked his mother.

"Oh yes! I remember those two things very well. I don't remember how many times I milked old Bossy, and I spent hours on that churn. My older sister almost always had something else to do, and my brother <u>claimed</u> he was too little," Mother reminisced.

"I think that is where I got my love for buttermilk," Adrian stated.

Adrian took little sips of that buttermilk off and on the rest of the evening.

As surprised as Mother and Father were...father spelled mother sitting with Adrian...they were glad Adrian was drinking something and keeping it down.

Adrian dozed off and on the rest of the evening. Mother decided to spend this first night in the room with Adrian. She wanted to be near her son, also she told herself that he was in a new place and would feel better with a familiar person in the room.

Adrian lay quietly thinking, "What an eventful day." That morning, he had awakened in the hospital, with the same-old, same-old. Then, in the space of one day, his world had turned upside down for the better. His emotions had been on a roller-coaster ride. Now, he was home in his own bed with new pajamas. His wonderful mother was right across the room, where he could see her any time, he wanted to. Boy, a fellow sure could never tell what could happen in one day. For just a moment, he wondered if he had made a wrong decision to want to come home. However, thinking about it, he felt that he had made the right decision by trusting the Lord. It was time to say his prayers, because he was getting sleepy again. He did not want to miss saying his prayers. He began as he usually did with the memorized prayers, realizing as always, how important they were. Then he prayed:

> *Dear Lord Jesus I thank You.*
> *It is so good to be home.*
> *Thank you for helping Mother and Father,*
> *To get this neat bed and great pajamas.*
> *Please bless my family,*
> *Especially my brothers and sister.*
> *I so glad I can drink buttermilk*
> *You know how much I already like it*
> *I feel there is something in it*
> *That You can use to help heal me*
> *Am I being weird to think of buttermilk?*
> *As kind of like medicine*
> *As always, You know what is best*
> *Please heal me, so I can be well,*
> *I ask it in your name,*
> *Lord Jesus,*
> *Amen.*

Adrian drifted off to sleep and began to dream. He was having another Angel Dream with what he now called, His Angel Friend. It was so great that in his dreams, he was a normal, healthy boy. This time, he was standing outside on a sidewalk, like the one he had seen briefly in the neighborhood where his new home was. It seemed to be just about dark. He was wondering how the grass got planted in the cracks in the sidewalk. He looked up as the His Angel flew down and landed gently beside him. He had taken to thinking of this angel as His Angel, called Silver Wing.

"Hello Adrian! How are you doing? Okay?" asked the Angel.

"I am doing just great Silver Wing. Did you come to talk to me again as my special friend? I always have such a neat time when I meet up with you."

"Well yes! I did come to see you, and yes, I am your friend." the Angel assured him.

"There is no stream to jump around here, but that sure was just about the best fun I ever had. Can we do something else like that? I like doing, what did you call it? Oh yeah! The impossible!" Adrian asked, after they had talked a while.

"Do you remember the secret to doing the impossible?" the angel asked.

"Let me think. Oh, now I remember. I had to put my hand in yours. Is that right?" Adrian questioned.

"Yes, that is it. Here, take my hand. How would you like to fly with me?" Silver Wing asked.

"Boy-oh-Boy! Boy-oh-Boy! Really! Can we do that? That would be fantastic. I always wanted to fly, ever since I was a little kid. Only not too high, or too fast. I don't want to go so fast I can't see anything, or too high for the same reason. But I like doing the impossible."

Adrian took Silver Wing's hand, and all of a sudden, he was flying. He looked down, and he could see houses and streets below. They were not flying too fast, so he could make out trees and bushes and stuff. They flew over places he recognized and saw things he knew. He saw a freeway with lots of cars and some trucks going both ways. Then they went as little higher up and flew over the city. There were lots and lots of lights, neon signs, traffic lights, and car lights and even some people walking on the sidewalks.

A lot of the buildings had the lights on. What if someone saw him flying? He had not thought of that. He looked down at his body and saw that he had his new pajamas on.

"I am not going to look at my pajamas. I don't think anybody can see me and this angel flying, and, even if they did, they would not believe their eyes." pondered Adrian.

"Can anybody see us way up here?" Adrian asked Silver Wing.

"Whose dream is this? "Asked Silver Wing.

"Well, it is my dream, I guess" claimed Adrian.

"Do you want anyone to see us?" was the next question.

"Well, no! I don't think that I do," Adrian replied.

"Well then, they cannot see you. You are the one in charge of this dream," Silver Wing assured him.

Things looked real pretty from up in the sky. He

saw a railroad track with a long freight train that stretched away in the distance. They flew along over the train as it crossed several railroad crossings, blowing that lonesome sound that freight trains have. It flashed into Adrian's mind the words from a railroad song.

It went something like, "You will know that I am gone when you miss the train I am on, you can hear that whistle blow one hundred miles, one hundred miles."

Railroad songs always seemed to be sad. Adrian guessed it was because all train whistles always sounded long and lonesome, especially at night.

"Stop thinking about train whistles and songs and think about flying," he told himself. Sometimes a wandering mind could interfere with, and get right in the way of, a fellow's thinking.

This was such fun. All too quick, the Angel brought Adrian back to the sidewalk where they started. For a couple of moments, Adrian was speechless. That did not happen too often. Then all he could say was "Boy-oh-Boy! Boy-oh-Boy!"

"It is time for me to go now. I had a good time! Did you?" Silver Wing asked, even though the answer was written all over Adrian's face.

"It was the most fantastic...the most super thing...I have ever done in my whole life." Adrian said. He was almost breathless with excitement. He felt like his heart was beating 90 miles a minute.

"I am glad," said Silver Wing. Then in a slightly more serious tone, he said, "There is another hint I want to tell you about the secret of doing the impossible. Your hand is like your trust." he said smiling.

"I don't understand that. It seems like you are always talking in riddles," Adrian answered, looking totally puzzled.

"You are such a big thinker. Think about it," the angel said, as he flew up in the air. He turned once and waved, then flew out of sight.

Adrian waved goodbye with both hands. His left hand, and arm was as good as his right. In fact, it was his left hand that he had put into the angel's hand. He realized this as he was standing on the sidewalk looking down at his hands. Suddenly, he woke up.

Adrian was back in his new bed. Boy, that dream sure seemed so real. He reached over and felt of his left arm with his right hand. The left side was still paralyzed. This was a harsh reality. But he decided instead of feeling sorry for himself, he would think about his dream. He lay awake for a little while, thinking about the angel and how much fun it had been flying. It had seemed so real. That dream, without a doubt, had been the very best dream he had ever had. It was not long, however, that the busy and exciting day got the best of him and he went fast asleep.

Country Hand Milk Churn

Chapter Twenty One
Day 69: [Thur.] First Day Home

Adrian woke and, for just a second, he did not know where he was. He took his right hand and pushed his head toward the room. Then in a flash, it all came back to him. He must have moaned or something, because his mother rose quickly from the armchair and hurried to his bedside.

"Good morning, Darling," she said cheerfully. "How do you feel this beautiful, bright morning?"

"I have a headache as usual. I hurt all up and down my right side and I still can't feel anything on my left side. Other than that, I am doing just fine," Adrian said, trying to be funny. Although his body was racked with pain and sickness his spirits were high this morning.

"I had quite a different night last night. Nobody came and stuck me with needles or woke me up to check my blood pressure or temperature," Adrian remarked.

"I dreamed about my angel friend again last night, Mother," Adrian said changing the subject.

"And what grand adventure did you have this time?" Mother asked. She was a little skeptical about his dreams, but they were only the dreams of a small boy immersed in a very difficult situation and facing almost insurmountable odds. What harm could they do? He always seemed in better spirits when he dreamed of **His Angel** as he called him. The Lord knows that he had little to be glad or happy about in his physical life lately.

"This time we went flying all over the city at night. We flew over a train and houses and the freeway and everything! Adrian claimed, getting excited. I even saw that store with the service station next door. You know, the one you shop at so you can get the S & H Green Stamps. Also, I saw a Jewel Tea home delivery truck at an all-night diner. Like that one that goes to Grandma Rose's House. The driver must have been getting him a burger and a cup of Java."

"That sure sounds exciting. Just like Superman, I bet," she commented.

"It was not quite like Superman. We did not go real fast. It was more like a fast floating, and I had to hold his hand. Also, I did not have a red cape or special suit like Superman. In fact, I was in my new pajamas. But it was one of the best times I have ever had. It seemed so real. And, Mother, I was well. Both my hands and feet worked. I was well again", he exclaimed.

"Mother, I seem to remember a real long time ago ridding on a train to Saratoga. Did we ever ride a train to Saratoga to visit Grandma Rose or Mam-Maw?" questioned Adrian. "Seeing that train made me think of it."

"Actually, we did make a couple of trips shortly after we moved to the Houston area. You were really young. It was before your sister was born. I am very surprised you still remember. They now have discontinued the run all the way into Saratoga, when the oilfield workers all moved out," Mother answered. She was always surprised with the things her son came up with. He seemed to associate the strangest things.

"Can I have some more buttermilk? I seem hungry again, a lot since I came home. That is a good feeling after not being able to eat for such long a time," Adrian pleaded.

"You can have all you want. I will get you a glass, then I have some work to do." Mother said, as she hurried out of the room to fetch it.

"That will be find, Mother. I may take a short nap after I drink some more buttermilk." Adrian called after her, as he was feeling a little sleepy.

The buttermilk was kept cool in the late model Ice Box that came with the house rental. The area had the convenience of an *Iceman*, who delivered ice twice a week on their street. Mother said that the way you notify the iceman how much ice you wanted is by putting a number in the front window, like, the number 25, for a twenty-five pounds block of ice. The ice company furnished a set of number signs for the sizes they had available. Ice usually took seven to eight days to melt. Of course, people needed to use wisdom, such as be sure the kids keep the door tightly closed, and let hot food cool, before putting it into the icebox, to name a couple.

Mother said the neighborhood ladies had told her that the iceman, was named Joe Rodriguez, and who served on their street, was really nice. And since he came right into their kitchens once or twice a week, they had become friends with him.

It was a fairly quiet neighborhood. Adrian woke from a short nap and heard someone mowing his or her yard with a push mower. You could not mistake that start and stop sound the rotary blades made. Some people were starting to get mowers that had gasoline engines, but they were still pretty expensive, and you had to pay 21 cents a gallon for gasoline.

Somewhere, Adrian heard children playing. It sounded like they were playing **kick the can** in the street. That made Adrian think about his brothers and sister coming home. Mother told Adrian that Aunt Stella May would bring Lee, Ann, home tomorrow. He was so anxious to see them. He heard what sounded like a lot of cars going up and down on the road behind the house. All in all, it was really quite a change from the hospital he had spent such a long a time in. His mother had turned on her favorite radio station that had, except for the news, recently started playing Christian music almost all day. It was not loud and kind of soothing in the background.

It seemed strange that he was able to get so much buttermilk down. At the end of the that day, Mother said he had drunk a whole pint since he got home, which was only about a day and a half. To Adrian, that seemed to be more than he had been able to swallow in the last two weeks.

His pain had mysteriously dropped to a level that he hardly noticed it, relative to what he had been used to. He had just a tingly kind of feeling in his left arm. For the most part, Adrian had spent a rather restful and uneventful day.

He skipped the memorized prayers but said his other stuff prayer being:

Dear Lord I want to Thank You,
For a great day at home.

I am glad I can drink the buttermilk,
It is good and I don't feel always hungry.
If I did any sin today
Will You forgive me.
Please bless Aunt Stella Mae,
Uncle John Boy and all my cousins.
Please bless Mother and Daddy
Please bless Lee, Ann, and
My baby brother Edmond.
Lord would you bless Polly
And Nurse Kincade and,
All the nurses that took care of me.
And I guess Dr. Billings, and
The Shadow, Dr. Jones.
Please help them to be nicer,
I think they need You in their heart.
Please bless all my country kin.
In Jesus Name I pray.
Amen!

Green Stamps   **Icebox**

Chapter Twenty Two
Day 70: [Fri.] The Kids Come Home

It was early Friday morning. The sun was just rising over Adrian's neighborhood. What a great idea, **Adrian's neighborhood**, thought Adrian. That was a perfectly delicious idea. It promised to be one of those outrageously beautiful sunrises, of which no two are ever exactly alike. The birds were singing their little hearts out. A gentle breeze ruffled the leaves in the big, old, oak tree in the front yard. Adrian saw through his windows, several squirrels playing chase in the yard. According to Father, they were not really **playing** chase. Father had read somewhere they were trying to establish their own territory. However, whatever they were doing, they seemed to be having a lot of fun doing it.

Adrian heard his father in the kitchen. Father grabbed a sack lunch and headed for work. He had landed a job at the airport, gassing the planes. He said he had already seen several important people. That, impressed him. Mother teased him, when she told him to listen closely and he might pick up some more "quotes." It was sort of game they played with each other. Because of his limited country education, he was impressed with important people and what they said. But he had little use for what he called "*a four flushe*r".

Father's favorite magazine was the National Geographic. He claimed even an old country boy like him could get a heap of learning, reading that magazine. He wanted all his children to finish high school and even go to college, if possible. He believed that you could do little to nothing about your beginning in life, but if you tried, you could do a lot about where you were going in life, with the **Good Lord's** help, of course.

Father stuck his head in the room where Adrian was and said, "Love you son! Glad you are home. See you after work."

A short while later, a knock at the front door announced the arrival of Uncle John Boy, Aunt Stella Mae, and the North children. His Aunt and Uncle decided a visit from all the cousins should be saved for another time, because a boy who was not expected to live two weeks should have looked like death warmed over. And they did not want to expose their children to that, just yet. Much to their surprise, Adrian did not look at all like what they expected to find. He was already looking much improved.

They all came into his room and, for a few minutes, there was a sort of bedlam. The adults asked Mother how he got to look so good. All she could say was "it is just the **Good Lord**." Both Lee and Ann sort of stood and stared at their brother.

After a while, Mother noticed the two children were kind of stand offish. Carrying the baby, she quietly pushed the other two closer to the Adrian's bed. "Say hello to your brother, you two!" she urged.

"Hello, Adrian," said Lee, sort of shyly at first.

"Hel-woe A-drwan," said the three-year-old Ann.

"Hello, y'all" Adrian said, as he waved with his left

hand, sort of feebly, but at least it moved. Which was a vast improvement over what it had been. He wanted to move it as much as possible.

"How have you been, Lee? Boy, I sure have missed seeing you and playing with you," Adrian said, grinning at Lee.

Lee was one who spoke what was on his mind. "I have missed you too. You sure are skinny. I bet you could get four or more pair of underwear under your jeans now." Lee had not forgotten the **grand spanking experiment.** Adrian was not the only blunt spoken one of the North Children.

"Yeah! I guess I am skinny. I am also very weak. I don't think I could punch my way out of a paper bag right now. You are going to have to wait a while before we have some good old wrestling matches again," Adrian said with a big grin, sort of wishfully.

Turning to Ann, Adrian asked, "You been a good girl, Red Head?"

"I be good, A-drwan," she answered with a giggle, "I been a weeell, good girl."

""Well, you are still the prettiest, red headed, freckle faced, sister a guy ever had in the whole wide world. "That's no brag, that's a fact!""

That last was a line Adrian used, that he had remembered from a western movie he had seen. He though it made him sound tough.

"And, how is my buddy, Edmond," Adrian asked, as his mother held the baby down where Adrian could see him up close.

The baby had no idea what all the excitement was

about. However, since everybody seemed to be happy and excited, he joined right in. He cooed, and gurgled, and laughed, right along with everybody else.

"Adrian still needs some peace and quiet," Mother said, as she gently ushered them all out of the room.

Adrian started to protest but then admitted, "I guess I am a little tired and sleepy."

The rest of the day was just wonderful for Adrian, He would daze off and then wake up. He could hear the family in the other part of the house. Every once in a while, either Lee or Ann would sneak off from the grownups and come into the room. Mostly they would just stare at this long-lost brother of theirs. For them, he had been gone so long. To them, he both looked the same, but yet somehow different. Anyway, they were sure glad he was back and that they could see and talk to him.

Every once in a while, his mother would come and check on him to see how he was doing. He asked for some more buttermilk, and she gave it to him. Lee wanted some also, and Mother gave in and gave him some. Ann said NO! when Mother teasingly offered her some.

Lee asked if he could stay and visit if he kept it quiet. Mother knew that the two boys might have a time keeping it quiet, but decided it would do no harm.

After Mother left, Adrian asked Lee, "So what has been going on? How do you like this house?"

"This house is so cool, after the last two places. This house came with an agitation washer with a hand crank wringer. So, Mother only has to wash the clothes, rinse them, then hang them out on the clothes line. There is a clothes line right in the back yard, with four lines on it. No more going to a laundromat like at the Cabins or using the old washer, rub board and wash tubs, like at the farm house."

"Father found a gas mower in the garage that the owner says Father can have if he wants it. It is broken so the last people who lived here just left it. Father told me it seems the only thing wrong, is the start cord is broken off and is bound up inside. He says it should be a snap to fix." "You know our Father can fix almost anything. I hope he does because, then you and I won't have to push an old rotary mower. Well, you won't any way, 'till you get healed and all better. You are going to get well, aren't you Adrian?" Lee asked in all sincerity.

"Yes, I believe **God** is going to heal me, and I will be all well." Adrian knew that his parents had not told the other children about the "death sentence" pronouncement by the doctors. They had told him not to say anything about it to them, either.

"Let me tell you something that is great fun." Lee said.

"So, tell me already," Adrian said, in anticipation!

"When the iceman comes, he has to stop in front of each house and enters in, to deliver the ice. All the guys, and even some of the girls, wait till he goes inside, then we run and get ice slivers off the back of the truck. Every time he chops out a block of ice, slivers go all over the back of his truck. That is so fun," Lee said, breathlessly.

"I can hardly wait," Adrian said, joining in the excitement.

"Adrian, how was it in the Iron Lung? I bet it was really scary. I prayed really hard for you 'till Mother told us you got out of it," Lee stated in all seriousness.

"It was scary and really bad, but I don't want to talk about it now. I will tell you all about it, sometime. Okay?" Adrian said, sort of chocked up.

"Sure, no problem," Lee saw Adrian's eyes, and quickly replied.

"You know what, I am glad you are back. I am tired of being responsible," complained Lee, changing the subject.

"But, being responsible is part of growing up," reasoned Adrian.

"Yeah! Well, that may be. But I am tired of when anything goes wrong around here, everybody always says I am responsible. You can start being responsible. You are the oldest," reasoned Lee.

"I get it," chuckled Adrian

When Father got off from work at the airport, he went over to a drugstore where his younger brother, Uncle Roy, now worked since he was out of the Army. He had a job working the soda counter. These counters had a bar-like serving area, with a long row of stools. The help could take your order and serve it, without ever leaving the work area. This drug store was so popular that they also had to put in a few tables. They also had a jukebox. They served mainly fountain drinks and ice cream and all the things you could build with ice cream, like banana splits, and such. The young teenagers had them create some strange concoctions. They also served cold sandwiches, such as BLT's. But no cooked sandwiches, like hamburgers.

Uncle Roy had an interesting story about when the owner hired him. The owner told Uncle Roy that he could eat all the ice cream he wanted. Uncle Roy helped himself for the first week or so, then hardly touched the ice cream. Then the owner told him after about a month, the reason for his **eat all you want policy**. He told Uncle Roy if he had said 'Don't eat the ice cream, or just a little now and then', the employee would keep helping himself a little at a time, as long as he worked there. With the **eat all you want policy**, the employee would pig out at the start, and then quit, which was exactly what Uncle Roy had done. So, in the long run the owner would save money on ice cream.

Father wanted to share with his brother about Adrian as well as pick up something to take home. Adrian had always loved cherry cokes, fountain coke cola with cherry syrup, also most ice cream. Father thought he would get some, to see if, by chance, Adrian could get it down as well. Also, he knew the other kids would love it. No Doubt! It would be a sort of family celebration for Adrian's home coming. He really wanted to achieve a feeling that he had made the right decision about taking Adrian out of the hospital and bringing him home. If not, he could perhaps create some pleasant memories of Adrian's last days, with family good times. It was a difficult decision he had made. His faith was strong, but it was not easy to go against the highly educated doctors.

When father got home with the cherry coke and ice cream, the family had a sort of party/celebration.

However, Adrian, try as he might, could only get a few swallows of any of it down. He really did appreciate the thought, and effort, and expense his father had spent to get it for him. He was also glad the other kids got a treat, but, try as he might, he just was not well enough yet to enjoy with them, this treat. He did believe in his heart that **God** would heal him, and he would soon be able to enjoy, along with the rest of them.

As the fun time was ending, Father did a rare thing for him. He told Adrian a country joke.

"Adrian, I have a question for you," with a grin, Father asked Adrian.

"Yes Sir," was the reply.

"What is the wisest critter in the forest?" Father asked.

"I do not know," Adrian replied.

"The owl, because he is the only one who gives a hoot" Father answered.

"Ha! Ha! That was a good one, Father. You seldom tell jokes," Adrian replied.

"Well, first of all, you don't know everything about your father. Also, most of the time, I don't feel like joking. But tonight, I am in a real good mood, and I know how much you like jokes," Father commented.

"Well, that was a good joke, and I think I will remember it always, because you told it to me," Adrian declared.

In his excitement Adrian skipped the Lord's prayer, quickly said the "Lay Me Down To Sleep" one and went to the other stuff prayer:

Here I am again, Lord.
This has been another great day.
Thank you for fixing it so,
I could be with my family.
I believe you are going to make,
Me all well so I can,
Enjoy good stuff,
Like we had today.
Please bless Mother and Father
And Lee, Ann, and Edmond.
I thank you Lord Jesus,
Such a great Family.
I am glad to learn,
My father can take time
To tell me jokes.
I know his life,
Is now and has been a hard one.
Please make it easier,
For him and all of us.
I want to ask you to please,
Forgive me all my sins,
Whatever I done did wrong.
<u>*In Jesus' name*</u>*,*
I ask it Lord, like that.
Cause that is the way,
The preacher and Father says,
We need to pray.
And Lord, in my other prayer,
I asked you my soul to keep,
While I sleep,
I ask you to keep it,

While I am awake also.
Amen.

Wash Tub Rub Board & Wringer

Hand Crank Wringer Washer

Chapter Twenty Three
Day 81: [Tues.] Bark Is Removed

Adrian woke by turning slowly in his bed. Mother had been letting him sleep 'till he woke up. Upon reflection, he realized he had a good night. Over the last two weeks he had gained strength. The paralysis had left him. But he still felt very weak.

His appetite had returned, and he was still drinking as much buttermilk as his mother would let him have. The usual fare that the family ate of beans, turnip greens, with buttermilk, and of course, taters, salmon patties, egg noodles and cheese...much better than the macaroni and cheese, that was so popular...and, for desert homemade biscuits and syrup...Log Cabin was the favorite brand they bought...all made Adrian anxious to get back to some real eating.

He was feeling much better and believed **God** had healed him. He realized that it was going to still be a long way to go before he was ready for that rough and tumble wrestling match with Lee, but he was sure looking forward to it.

Lee came in every day and talked with him and played in the room. Ann was still a little shy, but she would come and watch. If she saw Adrian watching her, she would get embarrassed and run from the room, giggling. Sometimes, Mother would take time from all her household chores and sit and talk with him for a few minutes. Father would often spend time with him after work.

The past few days had not been uneventful. He and his parents had gotten a lot of cards and letters from relatives as well as people in the church that they attended from time to time. Several people had come by for short visits. Some of these folks, Adrian had not seen in years. Aunt Lolla came by, but he somehow avoided her dreaded kiss. She did nail Lee, however.

"Why didn't you warn me she would do that? I could have disappeared when she got ready to leave," complained Lee when they were discussing it afterwards.

"Sorry Lee, I guess I did not think she would do it to you," had been Adrian's lame excuse.

"Yeah, right!" Lee had said.

Adrian realized that today was the day that Doctor Billings and Doctor Jones had prophesied that he would be dead by. Adrian guessed that maybe prophesied was too strong a word. However, they did say, or predict, that by this day he would be dead. He also realized that they predicted from their education and experience. They had not taken into account, the healing power of **Almighty God**. Adrian had hardly needed his glasses since he got home.

About midafternoon, everything had gotten quiet. Mother had decided today she would put Lee and Ann down for a nap. It was summer, so school was out. She decided it would be a good time to do some of the wash. She could go outside and hang out the clothes with only minimal watching over her household and kids. She left her radio on in the other room. Adrian heard a verse from a song that was playing softly. It was **"I can't even walk, Without You holding my hand"**

Adrian started thinking about his seemingly impossible plan, to get up and walk.

He felt God had healed him and, weak as he still was, it was time to prove it. Prove, once and for all, that he was healed. Perhaps it was a step of faith. All of a sudden, he remembered the secret that the angel in his dream had told him. To do the impossible, you had to put your hand in the hand of someone very powerful and strong. That last dream, the angel had said your hand is like your trust. So, like in the song, he needed to put his hand or trust in the hand of the **Lord Jesus. Jesus** could do the impossible.

If he was going to walk, he was going to have to trust **Jesus** to help him and not listen to any doubts or fears. Adrian prayed:

> *Lord Jesus, I am going to,*
> *Put my trust in You.*
> *Just liked I dreamed,*
> *What the Angel showed me,*
> *When I put my hand in his,*
> *I could jump a stream or fly.*
> *I am going to put my hand,*
> *Or trust in You Lord.*
> *I am going to get out of this bed,*
> *I am going to walk,*
> *Over to Mother's armchair.*
> *You have healed me.*
> *And not just to*

Lay in this bed.
Amen

Mustering all his strength, Adrian climbed over the rail along the side of his bed. He had not stood on his feet in over two months...about seventy-five days. By hanging on to the rail, he inched along the length of the bed. It took what seemed a very long time, and quite a lot of effort on Adrian's part. Several times, he felt his legs might collapse, and he would fall out onto the floor. He could not let that occur, no matter what happened.

At the end of the bed was his target, Mother's armchair. When he reached the end of the bed, he stopped to figure out how he was going to turn around and position himself to sit in the chair without falling on the floor. He paused to catch his breath.

Finally, he decided he would sort of push off from the bed, grab the arm of the chair, and do a swinging, turning move, and hopefully land sitting on the chair. He pushed and spun. His feet seemed to get all tangled up, but he made it. True, it was anything, but graceful. His behind was only partially on the seat cushion on the chair. The rest of him he flopped back into the chair.

He quickly sat up and scooted back into the chair. He rested his arms on the arms of the chair. He was very thankful to the **Lord** for his accomplishment. And, not a little pleased with himself. He knew his mother came into the room ever so often to check on him.

Sure enough, in a few moments, he heard his Mother come in the back door with an arm load of clothes off the clothesline.

Adrian smiled his biggest smile and said, "Look Mother, it has been two weeks, and I am not dead like the doctors said."

His mother dropped the clothes on the floor and grasped her hands to her breast. She then gently dropped to the floor, on her knees, and lifting her hands in the air, she began to weep tears of joy and gratitude to her Good Lord. Her son was indeed not only alive, but healed, and on his way to becoming a healthy, active, little boy again.

"Praise the **Good Lord**," was all she could say over and over.

A little later Adrian asked Mother if she could call Polly. Mother still had the number and after the second call, she reached Polly. She handed the phone to Adrian.

"Hello, Polly. This is Adrian," he said.

"**Adrian**! I am so glad to hear from you! How are you doing? Nurse Kincade told me how you left the hospital. I am so glad to hear from you." Polly repeated.

"Well, I am happy to report that the **Lord** has healed me. I no longer have polio. That is not from a doctor, but from the **Lord**. Today, with the help of the **Good Lord**. I got out of bed and walked. Not very pretty, I admit, but as I get my strength back, I believe I will soon be fully recovered," Adrian stated, in faith.

"Would you tell Nurse Kincade? She did her best and was a good and faithful nurse in a difficult job," Adrian asked.

"I am so thrilled for you, and, of course, I will tell Nurse Kincade," Polly answered.

"Polly, there was one more thing I would like to say to you," Adrian tentatively stated.

"Sure, what is that?" Polly questioned.

"You remember when I was explaining the country saying of **Life With The Bark On**?" Adrian asked.

"Yes, I remember," Polly replied.

"You remember what I said about the Log Cabin Ladies? That if they are going to live in the log cabin for an extended time, the ladies would clean up the inside of the cabin by peeling all the bark off the inside and sanding down the walls?" Adrian asked.

"Well, yes I do remember you saying something like that." Polly answered wondering where this was going.

"Well, Polly. The Lord has just peeled all the bark off the inside of the log cabin of my life, and I am going to stay, hopefully, for a long while," Adrian said.

The End

www.ingramcontent.com/pod-product-compliance
Lightning Source LLC
Chambersburg PA
CBHW071429070526
44578CB00001B/48